FOUNDATIONS OF MODERN POLITICAL SCIENCE SERIES
Robert A. Dahl, Editor

Public

Opinion

FOUNDATIONS OF MODERN POLITICAL SCIENCE SERIES

ENGLEWOOD CLIFFS, NEW JERSEY   Prentice-Hall, Inc.

R O B E R T   E.   L A N E

Yale University

D A V I D   O.   S E A R S

University of California, Los Angeles

FOUNDATIONS OF MODERN POLITICAL SCIENCE SERIES

Robert A. Dahl, Editor

C–73780 (*p*)   C–73781 (*c*)

Preface

Everyone, you will find, is an expert
on public opinion; after all he is a member
of the public and he knows how he feels
and what he thinks about an issue. Or does he? There is
a great deal about the way in which
people borrow opinions, or reach down into their
experience for guidance which is, even for the individual himself, out of sight. For example, most of us like to
think of ourselves as rational, independent-minded, critical
thinkers, forming our opinions on the basis
of a judicious consideration of the facts. We rarely
think of our opinions as being formed by group
memberships, forgotten childhood

v

experiences, party labels, friendship patterns. The message of this little book is that in many ways all of these are the same. It is a curious fact that one of the benefits of studying public opinion comes in the knowledge it gives to individuals about themselves. At least it gives them some ideas which they can use in examining their own opinion processes.

Yet, even if it were true that people were endowed with perfect self-knowledge, they might not understand what others were doing or thinking, or how they did these things. People differ in these respects; the middle-class college student may think the working-class man has the same values, information, and skills that he himself has; or the interested and alert young man may feel that his apathetic neighbor is basically like himself but only needs awakening. In many important respects this is not true. The study of public opinion, then, teaches something about the diversity of mankind, the many different ways in which people arrive at their judgments or opinions.

Our study deals mostly with the ways people arrive at their opinions—this, rather than exploring just what it is the public believes. We hope that understanding the mechanisms and processes of opinion formation provides a permanently useful set of tools for subsequent use by students, who like everyone else, forget data but may remember and use insights into how people behave.

There is one other matter to be said about the study of public opinion at this time, at least as we see the problem. We have observed that a great controversy seems to be going on about the question of autonomy versus conformity, group pressure and individual decision. Several of our chapters deal with this problem, for it is a bothersome one, not only for our time, but for other periods of history as well—and even for the understanding of the origins and workings of democracy. Perhaps, in some small way, our treatment can clarify public discussion of this issue.

We are indebted to many people, for, like the writers of most contemporary interpretations, we have relied heavily on the research done by many authors. Wherever possible, we have cited their work in the text; these citations should be read as part of our recognition of acknowledgment and gratitude to the many fine scholars in this field today. In addition, we wish to thank Robert Dahl, the Editor of this series, for his valuable suggestions, and James Murray and Wilbur Mangas of Prentice-Hall for their helpful assistance at every stage.

Robert E. Lane
David O. Sears

New Haven
Los Angeles
1964

Preface

Contents

viii

Contents

From Public Opinion to Public Policy?

CHAPTER ONE

Government policy, and, indeed, all important historical
events, are shaped by the opinions of the members of the political
communities involved. That is why we are interested
in public opinion. Shall the national government
pass a civil rights bill? Have the "warhawks" prepared us for
war? Shall the city issue bonds to pay for a new school?
The resolution of all of these issues is influenced
in one way or another by the sentiments of the public—although
the influence is often circuitous and hard to follow.

Areas of Public Opinion

Opinions have to be *about* something; the ones we are mainly interested in are about four things. First, they are about the political system, the regime, the constitutional framework, the way issues get decided. These opinions go to the root of things; disagreement on such matters can, if they are widespread, cause the system to break down. One of the main functions of public opinion in a going, stable regime is to provide a generalized support for the regime. Popular opinion provides effective legitimacy. Where this legitimacy is missing, the alienation of the disaffected can be expressed in (a) apathy and withdrawal—the more usual form—or, on occasion, in (b) the special politics of alienation—often destructive, irrational (in a sense we shall describe), and seemingly less interested in *what* is to be decided than in *who* will decide. Generalized support or alienated disaffection? This is the first question for public opinion and the first reason to be interested in it.

If, as in the United States, the question of the constitutional order is pretty well agreed upon by most people, a second subject for public opinion, in our consideration, is the question of the choice of group loyalties and identifications. Opinions cluster by groups: regional, national origin, race, religion, urban-rural status, and social class or status. Consciously or unconsciously people tend to identify with such groups as these (and many more specific ones: unions, trade associations, sporting clubs, and so forth) and to draw their opinions from these identifications. Politically, one of the most important of these group loyalties is loyalty to a political party. It is derived, in part, from sentiments toward the various social groups. And party loyalty is in many ways the most important single determinant of vote decisions in the United States. Although party loyalties have a life of their own, in the long run they are likely to be determined by whether the various social groups, which are more intimately related to people's daily lives, support one or another party. The pattern of loyalties to parties and other groups, then, is a crucial focus in the study of public opinion, for it affects the broadest policy orientations of government, gives strength to some group demands and not others, and directly affects the choice of leaders.

The choice of leaders itself is a third area of public opinion which attracts our attention. The public makes its selection only after the field has been narrowed down to a few of the many possible candidates, but the narrowing down is obviously done with public reaction in mind—and the final estimate by the public in its role as electorate is an important one. What kind of men do various elements of the public prefer? Strong, heroic types—as in the *personalismo* politics of the Latin-American republics? Men with certain "common-man" qualities whose reactions will be familiar and understood? Men whose social and occupational status makes it appropriate that they should hold "high office"? Public preferences and opinions on these matters shape public policy and the course of history in a variety of important ways.

2

Finally (fourth) there is the matter of public issues—topics, like the civil rights legislation mentioned above, or admission of China to the United Nations, or an embargo on Cuba, or aid to education by the federal government—on which some segment of the public has an opinion. These topics vary greatly in their power to attract attention and support or opposition; often the attentive public is rather small, and the informed public even smaller, but in the absence of strong opposition even a small public can make its influence felt. On the other hand, there is often a diffuse, badly informed, but intensely held set of opinions prevalent among a large public, a situation which poses a hazard for the better-informed political leaders. However these qualities of interest, intensity, and persuasion may be distributed, the issues which the course of history throws to the surface at any one time will find a resolution somehow shaped by public opinion.

Translating Opinion into Policy

The process of "shaping" is an enormously complicated one, but at the very least we can identify, if not completely explain, some of the ways in which this is done. The most obvious, of course, is the electoral process culminating in the vote. Here the ordinary members of the public, the people we are interested in in this book, experience a sense of choice and, for the most part, a feeling of influencing important events. Beyond that, there is the matter of writing letters and sending deputations to Congress or the State House or some other seat of power. Only about 10 per cent of the American public in any one year undertake this kind of activity. The act of joining, and therefore supporting, one or more of the many overlapping "interest-groups" in the United States gives force to some points of view, sometimes a point of view explicitly presented to civil servants and legislatures by lobbyists. This is also true, in a less obvious way, of the support given to certain media. Congressmen pay a great deal of attention to what the papers and television and radio commentators are saying. Papers with a wide circulation and programs with a considerable audience are, in a sense, made more powerful by their audiences. Then, too, there is the survey or poll respondent whose answers to questions on issues and men become part of a news report (or perhaps a private research report to the sponsoring official) revealing the current state of opinion—a condition which the wise official regards as partially plastic.

But the more we examine the influence of public opinion on policy, the more it seems desirable to stress the indirect influence, rather than the direct mandate theory, the idea that legislation perfectly reflects constituent opinion. Recent studies by the Survey Research Center at the University of Michigan have shown that there is a very tenuous relationship between the roll call votes of a congressman and the opinions of his constituents on a variety of issues: in long-established areas of controversy (such as social welfare legislation) there is a reasonably close correspondence—in foreign policy almost none. Moreover, in competitive districts there is much less correspondence between legislative views and popular

3

views than in less competitive districts—an odd and interesting finding in itself. As a consequence of this kind of new information, one is more likely to emphasize the influence of public opinion on the early shaping of the basic values and predispositions of political leaders, and the more informal and continuing "education" they receive in their daily contacts and life experiences in and out of office, in and out of their official roles. In many ways, it is the basic belief systems which these men develop in their pre-official lives which makes them responsive to the needs and values of their constituents—but this lies somewhat beyond the scope of our particular study.

The Scope of Inquiry

Americans, in particular, do not really doubt that public opinion is influential in the shaping of events. The interesting questions come in refining our understanding of this process—something we shall attempt to do in this small volume. We will begin, in the next chapter, by outlining the nature of an opinion (public or private) so that we will have a clearer picture of what we are talking about. Then, in the following three chapters, we will discuss the formation of such opinions: how they are often first acquired in the home, and then gradually changed by experience; how group memberships exert their subtle but powerful pressures; how political and other leaders shape people's opinions. Finally, in the remaining chapters, in what is the most controversial part of this study, we take up four problems of public opinion which have been much argued over in recent times. One of these is the set of problems implied by the low level of information and the poor quality of thought applied to political matters. Another, closely related, problem is the confusing issue of rationality in politics. A third problem has to do with conformity—is it such a bad thing, after all? And fourth, we discuss some aspects of emotional intensity in politics. How shall we achieve a political style which carries conviction but not fanaticism? And what shall we do about the intense minority and the apathetic majority?

4

From Public Opinion to Public Policy?

Portrait
of an Opinion

CHAPTER TWO

Miss Sherwin of Gopher Prairie, says Walter Lippmann,
is trying to understand the news reports
on the First World War. "She has never been to France, and
certainly she has never been along what is now the battlefront. Pictures
of French and German soldiers she has seen, but it is impossible
for her to imagine three million men. . . . Miss Sherwin has
no access to the order of battle maps, and so if she
is to think about the war, she fastens upon Joffre and the Kaiser
as if they were engaged in a personal duel.

Perhaps if you could see what she sees with her mind's eye, the image in its composition might be not unlike an eighteenth century engraving of a great soldier. He stands unruffled and more than life size, with a shadowy army of tiny little figures winding off into the landscape behind."[1] How shall we analyze Miss Sherwin's opinions, and the opinions of the public of which she is so significant a part?

Lane asked O'Hara, a sprightly little mechanic in Eastport, "What groups do you think have the most influence on city politics?" First he frowned and then he smiled: "Oh [pause] labor has something to do with it—there's no doubt about that; your Knights of Columbus, your Masons, and things like that. They've got a lot to do with it, because, as it is, the higher you get up in the Knights, or you get up in the Masons or something, you're more or less up there—you're pulling a lot more weight there. Your veterans' organizations have a lot to do with it, too—like your American Legion and that. The American Legion has a lot to do with it, not only in the city, but all over—they pull a lot of power."[2] O'Hara is a lot closer to city politics than Miss Sherwin is to the battlefronts, but like her, he must pull together a lot of vague impressions, organize them, and formulate an opinion.

An opinion, we will say, is "an implicit verbal response or 'answer' that an individual gives in response to a particular stimulus situation in which some general 'question' is raised."[3] It may or may not be overtly expressed; Lane asked O'Hara to express his opinions, but perhaps he had a private opinion on the power of these groups before it came up in this way and perhaps he had some opinions he did not care to tell his interviewer. In reading the paper Miss Sherwin may have been formulating opinions which she never had a chance to express. But if they are expressed, or implied, so that an analyst can see them, how shall we describe them?

Describing an Opinion

The two dimensions which public opinion analysts most commonly use to describe an opinion are *direction* and *intensity*.

DIRECTION

When we say an opinion has direction, we mean that it includes some affective or emotional quality of approving or disapproving of something. It has a "pro-con" quality. Miss Sherwin is pro-Joffre and anti-Kaiser in their duel, and O'Hara says, in a later passage, that he trusts the veterans' organizations more than most groups. Stated or implied, this pro-con quality is almost always there.

If direction tells us, in effect, "yes" or "no," what shall we do with

[1] Walter Lippmann, *Public Opinion* (New York: Penguin, 1946), p. 8.

[2] For further interpretation of the opinions of urban working men, see Robert E. Lane, *Political Ideology: Why the American Common Man Believes What He Does* (New York: The Free Press of Glencoe, 1962).

[3] Carl I. Hovland, Irving L. Janis, and Harold H. Kelley, *Communication and Persuasion* (New Haven: Yale University Press, 1953), p. 6.

"maybe" or "it depends"? These are, in effect, requests by the respondent for new "questions" with greater specificity so that he may qualify his commitment, avoiding a "yes" or "no" answer. This is the purpose of a "qualified answer." In general, the analysis of opinions should include this matter of "qualification," since it gives us a more detailed picture of the psychic disposition of the opinion holder, but it is not easy to get at. Moreover, it is more difficult to categorize respondents if each gives a slightly different answer.

Some groups of people tend to qualify answers more than others: Educated people give more "qualified" answers than do those with little education; and intensity of feeling, as one might expect, tends to discourage qualification. Oral answers, too, tend to bring out qualifications more than do written communication. Qualification serves something of a protective function in the face-to-face situation; also, the ease of expression tends to make the longer qualified statement less of a burden.[4]

Under some circumstances, there are tendencies to give mostly pro or mostly con answers regardless of the content of the question. For example, the Lynds say that the Middletown spirit supports "being loyal, and a 'booster,' not a knocker."[5] Lane finds that the concept of good citizenship in Eastport emphasizes "supportive" rather than "critical" attitudes.[6] "Accentuate the positive" says a song popular in the 'forties. Perhaps a culture can shape the attitudinal direction of a people so that, compared to others, they express opinions more in one of these directions than another.

But if the culture emphasizes the positive in some important respects, perhaps this is not true of the area of culture most fraught with conflict—politics. It is said, for example, that in politics, each candidate spends so much time criticizing his opponent that observers come away with a totally negative impression (in contrast, for example, with advertising, where each product is eulogized since it is illegal to disparage an opponent's product, and observers presumably come away with a totally positive impression). Actually, this is not the case. In one study of a California election—a hard fought one, at that—only 25 per cent of the candidates' total public references were critical of the opposition.[7] But still, people might be more likely to vote *against* the opposition than *for* the candidate and party they favor. This seems to vary a great deal. In Boston, local elections seem to be of this kind; voters look for the candidate who will do the least harm.[8] Roper states that in New York in 1945, in reply to queries on why persons were voting for their respective candidates (O'Dwyer, Morris, Goldstein), he received only vague and unpersuasive answers such as a man's "good experience" or "his good record." But this

[4] Deane Neubauer, Carolyn Pratt, Elinor J. Rubens, and John Thomas, "An Introduction to Political Conversation," unpublished paper, 1963.

[5] Robert S. and Helen M. Lynd, *Middletown in Transition* (New York: Harcourt, Brace, 1937), p. 404.

[6] Lane, *op. cit.*, pp. 161–186.

[7] Galen Rarick, *California Daily Newspaper Reporting of the 1950 U.S. Senatorial Campaign: A Content Analysis* (M.A. Thesis, Stanford University Library, 1951), as summarized in Stanford University News *Press Releases*, January 26, 1951.

[8] Murray B. Levin, *The Alienated Voter* (New York: Holt, Rinehart and Winston, 1960).

Portrait of an Opinion

was not true of answers to his queries about why people voted against the opposition candidate. Here the replies were informed and emotional, suggesting that more thought and attention went into these negative aspects of voting than went into the endorsements implied in a positive vote.[9] But in national politics, at least in 1952, when asked to talk about the good and bad points of the two candidates, the average person was able to enumerate more good than bad attributes in these political aspirants.[10] The tendency to be generally "pro" or generally "con" is one of several possible "response sets"; that is, a fixed tendency to answer all questions in a certain way. There seems generally to be a more positive "response set" toward national political leaders than local political leaders. Like the valet who knows his master best, the public may be most critical of those whose governing is closest to them.

Another aspect of this matter is whether or not systematic differences exist between persons in terms of their tendencies to give pro or con answers, regardless of the question. Of course, the distinction between "boosters" and "knockers" has been current in popular discourse for a long time, but only recently has this idea of "response sets" been systematically measured. We still do not know very much about it, but one recent study concludes that the difference between "Yeasayers" and "Naysayers" reflects basic personality dynamics. The findings of this study suggest "that the best single characterization of the traits associated with agreeing response set is *Stimulus Acceptance* vs. *Stimulus Rejection*. The yeasayer accepts stimuli both by admitting them to consciousness without censorship, alteration, or assimilation and by agreeing with, acting out, and otherwise yielding to the pressures of stimuli exerted on him. The naysayer tends to reject these same stimuli."[11] Milbrath took this notion and tried it out on some data he had on Washington lobbyists and a national election study. He found that those who had a positive response set tended to be Democrats and those with a negative response set tended to be Republicans —a pattern with relatively low but statistically significant correlations. This was especially true in the national election study of those Democrats whose fathers were non-partisan, that is, who arrived at their party identification more on the basis of their own choice than of simple inheritance. One reason for this, he discovered, was that there was a low but positive and significant correlation between a liberalism or "social welfare" scale and the yeasaying tendency. Nor could any of these relationships be explained away on the basis of education or social status, although these factors weakened the relationship where they could be applied.[12] However, this proposition needs further research support before it can be regarded as conclusive.

[9] Elmo Roper, "New York Elects O'Dwyer," *Public Opinion Quarterly*, Vol. 10 (1946), pp. 53–56.

[10] Angus Campbell, Gerald Gurin, and Warren Miller, *The Voter Decides* (Evanston, Ill.: Row, Peterson, 1954), pp. 53–54.

[11] Arthur Couch and Kenneth Keniston, "Yeasayers and Naysayers: Agreeing Response Set as a Personality Variable," *Journal of Abnormal and Social Psychology*, Vol. 60 (1960), p. 170; see also "Agreeing Response Set and Social Desirability" by these same authors in the same *Journal*, Vol. 62 (1961), pp. 175–179.

[12] Lester W. Milbrath, "Latent Origins of Liberalism-Conservatism and Party Identification: A Research Note," *Journal of Politics*, Vol. 24 (1962), pp. 679–688.

In summary, then, the first thing to understand about an opinion is its direction. Both individual personality patterns and culture may produce general dispositions to give positive answers or negative answers, more or less independent of the content of the question.

INTENSITY

People feel very strongly about certain of their opinions, much less strongly about others. Thus, in inquiring about their opinions it makes sense to ask people to specify the intensity of their feeling. For example, in 1956 the Survey Research Center presented its respondents with the following statement: "The government ought to help people get doctors and hospital care at low cost." And it asked them to reply in these terms: "agree strongly, agree not very strongly, not sure, it depends, disagree but not very strongly, disagree strongly." The first and last are of course the most intense responses.

Intensity is also an important dimension of loyalty to groups. After asking people to report which party they generally favored, the SRC interviewers asked them: "Would you call yourself a strong (Republican) (Democrat) or a not very strong (Republican) (Democrat)?" In general people do not have much trouble stating how strongly they feel about opinions of these kinds.

When an issue becomes a moral question, it generally draws very intense opinions. However, both Riesman and Lane[13] have reported that Americans (as they have interviewed them) rarely tend to be indignant about public affairs or to convert them into great moral issues. On the face of it this seems very different from much European and, indeed, world-wide political behavior. If Americans truly differ in this respect, it explains a great deal of what is unique in American politics and deserves further exploration. We shall do this in a later chapter.

THE PUBLIC OPINION CONTEXT

The direction and intensity of an opinion are the attributes used by most analysts to place it in the public opinion context. That is, they are used to determine where an individual stands in relation to public opinion generally on the issue. But it is not a simple matter to settle upon a description of the public opinion context, or upon the most important attributes of that context. Such a description must follow from the assumption that within a given population (all Americans of voting age, for example) there is a given distribution of opinions. Therefore one must first place an individual's opinion in its relation to this population distribution. The following are some of the more common ways of doing so:

1. *The modal opinion.* We can determine which position is modal within the population; i.e., which opinion is held by the most people. The interest among students of government focused on the problem of "con-

13 David Riesman, *The Lonely Crowd* (New Haven: Yale University Press, 1950); Lane, *op. cit.,* pp. 321–345.

9

sensus" and the interest among sociologists in the problem of "deviance" suggests some of the reasons why this aspect of an opinion is important.

If there is only one mode, as in the case of opinions toward universal suffrage, the issue cannot be described as highly controversial. However, sometimes public opinion is bimodal; that is, there are two very popular, and opposed, positions. And sometimes there are several modal positions; in the case of federal aid to education in the early 1960's, many congressmen were simply opposed to aid on principle, others supported it only if it were extended to private and parochial schools as well as to public schools, others supported it only if it was *not* extended to parochial schools, others supported it only if it was not extended to segregated school systems, and so forth. There were, in fact, so many modes within the critical population (United States representatives) that the issue could not be defined even in terms of two very popular but opposed positions. In such cases, of course, it is difficult to get action.

2. *Extremity*. Given a population distribution of opinion, some positions can be regarded as "extreme" and others as "moderate." Whether a person has an "extreme" position or a "moderate" position therefore depends very much on how the population as a whole regards the matter. For example, a person in Nazi Germany who advocated publicly identifying Jews but not treating them in a discriminatory fashion would not be regarded there as an extreme anti-Semite. A person taking the same position in the United States today would, of course, be regarded as an extreme anti-Semite.

So-called "extremist" opinions are not so designated merely on the basis of their places within the population distribution of opinions. Such opinions are usually considerably more intense than the average. Extremity and intensity are not the same, of course, since extremity locates a position on a continuum of possible positions, while intensity tells how strongly a person feels about it. Nevertheless, empirically it has been well established that on most issues there is a U-shaped curve relating the two. The more extreme a person's position is—say, on desegregation, where immediate total integration is one extreme and total and absolute segregation is the other—the more intensely he is likely to feel about his opinions.

These questions of modality and extremity are at the heart of a problem which seems to be racking the intellectual community these days— the problem of conformity. We shall return to this later.

STABILITY

Like some aspects of the opinions we have discussed above, stability refers more to the opinion holder than to the opinion itself. It raises the question whether, at some future point in time, the direction and intensity of an opinion will be substantially the same. Since the discussion of the formation of an opinion and the problem of persuasion treated in later chapters deals with this aspect in some detail, we will not enter into a further exploration here.

10

We have been describing an opinion as if it consisted merely of one "answer" to one "question." Actually, of course, a person generally has a variety of different "answers" which he can give to a particular question. The entire cluster of opinions a person has about a particular topic can be described in several important ways.

INFORMATIONAL CONTENT

As everyone knows, there are informed opinions and uninformed opinions. Smith, Bruner, and White observe that "informational support" does not refer so much to the opinion itself as "the amount of the available information that may go into the building of" the opinion,[14] but the two are so closely allied, they should be treated together. One of the most interesting aspects of opinion on public affairs is the degree to which people will hold rather "strong" views on matters on which they have almost no information; the intensity of opinion coming from some symbol, such as "flag" or the word "Constitution," or from some reference group, such as "Irish" or "southerner," rather than from a reasoned view of probable consequences of a course of action.

One of the criteria of an informed opinion is the degree of *differentiation* employed; that is, the discrimination among events or people or issues in a way relevant to the opinion. The lumping together of all forms of government enterprise (Post Office, public irrigation, TVA) as "creeping socialism" or the stereotyping of all Negroes in a single bundle of traits represent the failure of differentiation. A person with a highly differentiated opinion is usually more aware of alternative responses.[15]

A second kind of information is the awareness of the *implications* of an opinion. Polls have shown that almost everyone supports the idea of free speech, but few people understand that this implies granting people holding positions they particularly dislike the right to speak. Thus in a study of Ann Arbor, Michigan, and Tallahassee, Florida, more than a third of the respondents would deny the right of free speech for "someone who wanted to speak in this city against churches and religion."[16] Under these circumstances one would say that those who supported the idea of free speech and the Bill of Rights, but denied its implications, were uninformed. We shall return to this later, for the great discrepancy between what seems to be expected of the public and what it is in fact capable of doing raises considerable doubts, not about democracy, which seems fairly healthy in America, but about our theory of the representative process.

[14] M. Brewster Smith, Jerome S. Bruner, and Robert W. White, *Opinions and Personality* (New York: Wiley, 1956), p. 36.

[15] P. F. Lazarsfeld, "The Controversy over Detailed Interviews—An Offer for Negotiation," *Public Opinion Quarterly*, Vol. 8 (1944), pp. 38–60.

[16] James W. Prothro and Charles M. Grigg, "Fundamental Principles of Democracy: Bases of Agreement and Disagreement," *The Journal of Politics*, Vol. 22 (1960), pp. 276–294.

11

Another important characteristic of an opinion cluster is its degree of organization. First, the degree of *integration* or *isolation* of various opinions is often of importance. The extreme ideologue may have a set of opinions all of which are continually referred one to another. A citizen with poorly organized opinions may, on the other hand, hold several which are clearly relevant to each other, but which he has never thought of in connection with each other. Jeanne Watson, in a study of opinion changes toward Negroes and others showed that while some of these attitudes were congruent with basic supporting attitudes, others were at odds with the basic features of a person's social outlook. The latter group of attitudes, of course, were more vulnerable to attack, less stable.[17] Hence the degree of intercommunication of relevant opinions is an important attribute of an opinion cluster.

A second significant characteristic of an opinion cluster is the notion of *breadth*. One might ask for example, whether prejudice toward Negroes is an exception to a generally tolerant view of other people or, as is more likely, is a part of a broad ethnocentrism: the tendency to reject others ethnically not like oneself. The study called *The Authoritarian Personality*, by Adorno and others, showed that anti-Semitism was often part of a broadly ethnocentric view of others. This study also revealed that prejudiced people have an even more general tendency first to sort out people into an admired in-group and a disliked out-group and second to assign a "higher" or a "lower" place to everyone so that the world appeared as a kind of general status hierarchy.[18]

Finally, in this explication of "organization" there is Lazarsfeld's idea of "frame of reference."[19] Within what scheme of values, he asks, is an opinion held? For example, in Lewin's study of diet changes during World War II—a study which revealed that only when a person achieved a certain economic security did he view diet as a matter of health more than a matter of budget—opinions on diet were influenced by such values as money or health.[20]

The organization of an opinion cluster has a great deal to do with the problem of rationality, to which we shall return later.

An attribute closely related to organization is the degree of internal consistency among the constituent opinions in an opinion cluster. In the extreme case, a paranoid schizophrenic, who is incapable of representing the world as it is, often has a set of opinions which are completely consistent

[17] Jeanne Watson, "Some Social and Psychological Situations Related to Change in Attitude," *Human Relations,* Vol. 3 (1950), pp. 15–56.

[18] T. W. Adorno, Else Frenkel-Brunswik, Daniel J. Levinson, and R. Nevitt Sanford, *The Authoritarian Personality* (New York: Harper, 1950).

[19] Lazarsfeld, "The Controversy over Detailed Interviews—An Offer for Negotiation," *op. cit.,* pp. 38–60.

[20] Kurt Lewin, "Forces Behind Food Habits and Methods of Change," cited in Lazarsfeld, *ibid.*

Portrait of an Opinion

with each other. He may claim to be the top administrative officer of his hospital, and can answer any other question about his situation in a way which is consistent with this assumption. It can be a most discouraging and lengthy task to try to catch him up in inconsistencies. At the other extreme are many citizens who rarely think about political matters. They often hold several opinions which are clearly inconsistent with each other, but they have thought about them so little, and expressed them so rarely, that the inconsistencies are not sources of discomfort, and are often not even noticed.

One reason why people hold inconsistent opinions is that they have different opinions for different social situations. According to the definition of an opinion given earlier, an opinion is an "answer" that is given to a "question" in a given situation. When the question *or* situation varies somewhat, a somewhat different response can be expected. Differences in the wording of questions often give quite different results, as the following examples show. In June, 1941, when asked whether they favored the United States entering the war against Germany and Italy or staying out, 29 per cent of one sample of the public said that they favored American entry. But when a similar sample was asked this question with several other options, such as supplying Britain with war materials, only 6 per cent favored entering the war against Germany and Italy (American Institute of Public Opinion, May, 1941). What is the "true" opinion? The question makes no sense because the alternatives brought to the attention of the respondents are different in each case. Similar findings were reported by Payne in a study of attitudes toward public health insurance. He found that in one poll in which a sample was asked its opinion on extending the social security laws to cover doctor and hospital care, 68 per cent of the sample supported this idea. When another similar sample was asked if it favored medical insurance supported by the private insurance companies, 70 per cent of the respondents supported *this* idea. Finally, when a sample was forced to choose between the two positions, 35 per cent favored governmental medical insurance, and 31 per cent favored private medical insurance, with the remainder either indifferent or not offering an opinion.[21]

THE POLICY COMPONENT

The problem of inconsistencies in a person's opinions on a given topic, stemming from differences in stimulus situations, comes up most frequently in connection with discrepancies between verbally expressed opinions and action. A person may express one opinion verbally (e.g., Negroes should be allowed to live where they please) but not behave consistent with that opinion (e.g., actively oppose a Negro's moving in next door). One's analysis of such inconsistencies depends upon one's view of opinions generally.

At the very beginning of modern public opinion research, Floyd Allport suggested that public opinions "are in the nature of present efforts

[21] Stanley L. Payne, "Some Opinion Research Principles Developed Through Studies of Social Medicine," *Public Opinion Quarterly*, Vol. 10 (1946), pp. 93–98.

Portrait of an Opinion

to oppose or accomplish something."[22] Much later Smith, Bruner, and White said that one important aspect of an opinion (and its holder) was the "policy stand" implied. This may or may not reflect a person's exact personal preference, they said, but it does reveal his estimate of what, given all the circumstances, the responsible authority should do about a situation.[23] Both Allport and Smith, Bruner, and White emphasize the policy resolution of a situation as a feature of opinion. This refers to what others should do about it, but one might equally include reference to what "I" the opinionholder, should do about it—that is, the implied activity of the opinionholder. Since some people act out their beliefs, and others merely verbalize them, this dimension can be an important one in sorting out types of opinionholders.

Some kinds of opinions seem "actionable" while others are not. Cantril says, in reference to opinions during World War II: "Opinions upon which concrete judgments and actions are based, often appear to go contrary to opinions abstractly held, since the latter are purely intellectual data that either call for no concrete action or offer no possibility of concrete action."[24] An example of the difference between an abstract opinion and an opinion guiding behavior is presented in La Piere's now classic and rather simple study. He traveled throughout the United States with a Chinese couple, stopping at 66 sleeping places and 184 eating places. On only one occasion were the Chinese couple refused service. At the conclusion of the trip, La Piere sent a questionnaire to the proprietors of these hostelries asking if they would accept members of the Chinese race as their patrons. He received negative replies from 92 per cent of the sleeping places and 93 per cent of the eating places.[25]

One view that is often taken toward the relationship between verbally expressed opinions and overt behavior is that the former is a predictor of the latter. The frequency of such inconsistencies between the two, as illustrated in La Piere's study, renders this an inadequate view. Rather, it is likely that the individual has several opinions which may be more or less conflicting, in a logical sense; each is held sincerely but limited to a specified stimulus situation. A legislator may vehemently oppose relief payments to the poor, but, placed in an administrative position, be unwilling to deny aid to a particular indigent family. In short, there may or may not be close correspondence between verbally expressed opinions and overt behavior. The two situations make different requirements upon the individual, and draw different sets of responses from him. It is a mistake to say that the individual is hypocritical or that the opinion measures are unreliable if the two do not correspond exactly. Any two situations may assess different aspects of the individual's cluster of opinions on a given issue.

22 Floyd Allport, "Toward a Science of Public Opinion," *Public Opinion Quarterly*, Vol. 1 (1937), pp. 7–23.
23 Smith, Bruner, and White, *op. cit.*, p. 37.
24 Hadley Cantril, "Opinion Trends in World War II: Some Guides to Interpretation," *Public Opinion Quarterly*, Vol. 12 (1948), p. 41.
25 R. T. La Piere, "Attitudes vs. Actions," *Social Forces*, Vol. 13 (1934), pp. 230–237.

Portrait of an Opinion

Finally, particular opinions, or particular opinion clusters, differ with respect to their salience. Pollsters often wish to find out what opinion clusters are most salient, as a way of finding out what issues people are most concerned about. For example, in a national study called *Communism, Conformity, and Civil Liberties,* people were asked "What kinds of things do you worry about most?" The answers showed that "The number of people who said that they were worried either about the threat of communists in the United States or about civil liberties was, even by the most generous interpretation of occasionally ambiguous responses, *less than 1%.*" When pushed to remember additional "worries," 6 per cent mentioned communism.[26] Compared with other worries, most of which had to do with personal problems, the threat of communist subversion in America was not salient.

Salience, then, means relatively important, at the focus of attention, crowding out other items, a pivot for organizing one's thoughts and acts. It changes, of course, according to one's tasks and situation, according to the news and the conversation one is exposed to, but it also has an enduring quality.

Different opinions may vary in their salience within an opinion cluster, as well. For example, at election time, some opinions are highly salient, while others do not seem to be particularly outstanding. Election decisions must encompass attitudes toward at least two candidates, usually two political parties, a variety of issues, and a set of group loyalties. Sometimes attraction toward one candidate is salient, and overcomes contrary attitudes in other areas—this seemed to be the case with many Democrats who preserved their party loyalty but voted for Eisenhower in 1952 (about 25 per cent of the 1948 Democrats switched this way).[27] But, as it turns out, in most elections, for most people, party loyalty is the most salient feature of this attitudinal complex.

In non-election situations salience also determines which of a cluster of opinions is to be the dominant or pivotal one. In studying attitudes toward Russia, M. Brewster Smith found that one reason most over-all appraisals were so negative, was because "The aspects in regard to which Russia was likely to be viewed with relative favor turn out only rarely to have had determinative importance for the respondents."[28] Thus, even if a respondent said that there was more economic security in the Soviet Union than in the United States, economic security, as contrasted with "liberty" or "opportunity" had little salience in the attitudinal complex.

There are other qualities of opinions and opinion clusters which are sometimes useful in analyzing public opinion: opinions may be *personal-*

[26] Samuel A. Stouffer, *Communism, Conformity, and Civil Liberties* (Garden City, N.Y.: Doubleday, 1955), pp. 59, 70.

[27] Campbell and others, *op. cit.,* p. 16.

[28] M. Brewster Smith, "The Personal Setting of Public Opinions: A Study of Attitudes Toward Russia," *Public Opinion Quarterly,* Vol. 11 (1947–48), p. 510.

Portrait of an Opinion

ized in the sense that they focus on the actors, not the events; they may be *moralized* in the sense that they tend constantly to bring moral judgments to bear on issues; they may be *mystified*, in the sense that they tend to suggest mysterious forces at work, things incomprehensible to the human mind or secret group working behind the scenes. But here we have focused on the main descriptive dimensions: the direction and intensity of a particular opinion, and the organization, informational base, consistency, and policy components of an opinion cluster. We shall return to some of these later, in our analysis of certain problems of public opinion in the American political system. But first we must examine how opinions are learned and changed.

Forming
and Weakening
the Parental
Opinion
Tradition

Recent research into the nature of political man
has come upon the same discovery that marked Freud's research
into human nature: Political life, like sexual life, starts much
earlier than we had thought. This is an important discovery
because the task of shaping political man is complicated and to
be effective must take account of the earliest
beginnings. In a system like a democracy, where many
people must be trained for participation
and responsibility, a set of delicate balances

must be established—balances of traits within and among men. As a result, men must be loyal to their political community and nation without becoming chauvinists. They must support its (democratic) values, but be tolerant of an examination of these values by critics. Political leadership and authority must have popular respect and often obedience, but members of the public must reserve some qualities of independence and autonomy. They must be partisans of the groups that sponsor their interests (political parties, unions, trade associations), but it should be a critical partisanship. Some of them must be intensely interested in public affairs and most should be somewhat interested, but even those most interested should have other interests and values. Interest and partisanship imply a responsibility for being informed (informed men are often opinion leaders), but information needs digestion, thought, application to problems in a strategy of efficient action. Now, we find that in order to effect these highly civilized balances in young citizens, we cannot wait until high school or college, for political orientation has already begun in grammar school.

First let us examine the development of political consciousness in the American child in terms of consensus: When, and how does he learn the consensual basis of American politics—those orientations and opinions upon which almost all American children seem to agree?

The Political Acculturation of the American Child

The child's opinions about politics, like his opinions on religion, are close reflections of his parents' views. The first and basic training he receives is in the family. Here he learns attitudes toward authority, toward others, toward himself, toward a vague outside community and nation. He learns habits of thought and behavior: independence, conscientiousness, trust. Let us examine, as a kind of baseline, the political orientations of these broad kinds discovered in several studies in the United States.

First, with respect to the most general orientation, an attitude toward the society outside the home, the political community and nation, Easton and Hess report an early positive sense of trust and support. On the basis of an examination of the responses of some 700 school children in the Middle West, they say, "The sentiments of most children with respect to their political community are uniformly warm and positive throughout all grades, with scarcely a hint of criticism or note of dissatisfaction."[1] "America" as a symbol and as a designation of their own country becomes suffused with this positive emotion. More than that, it becomes confused with religion for "not only do many children associate the sanctity and awe of religion with the political community, but to ages 9 or 10 they sometimes have considerable difficulty in disentangling God and country."[2] As these authors note, such a strong affective tie to country creates a bond which is likely to last a lifetime. They might also have observed that it lays the groundwork for a more dangerous view: "my country right or wrong." The

[1] David Easton and Robert D. Hess, "The Child's Political World," *Midwest Journal of Political Science*, Vol. 6 (1962), pp. 236–237.
[2] *Ibid.*, p. 238.

Forming and Weakening the Parental Opinion Tradition

Easton and Hess findings thus suggest the reason for Litt's finding that from a fifth to a third of some Boston area high school students could be classified as "very" chauvinistic.[3]

Attitudes toward authority represent another basic common orientation. Greenstein's study of some 659 preadolescent school children in New Haven reveals in this respect, too, a positive, supportive, uncritical view of political life. These views are developed in the earliest years not on information about what the President or the Mayor does, but on purely emotional grounds; later, of course, these opinions become somewhat more informed and critical but they retain this positive tone.[4] For example, Hess and Easton find that the President retains, with older school children, his favorable image in his job-related qualities, but he tends to lose his overwhelming advantage as a moral or sociable person.[5] The results of both studies indicate that the positive affective or emotional components of these opinions develop prior to cognitive elaboration about their objects; put another way, information follows evaluation, rather than preceding it, in the course of the child's development.

Like the findings on love of country, these overwhelmingly trusting views of the President (and the Mayor too) might cause political theorists to worry. Such trust forms an ideological bridge for loyal citizenship, but might it not also foster overly dependent and uncritical attitudes toward authority? Apparently not. Not only does the American adult have a generally restrained and balanced view of political authority,[6] but when American students are compared with German and Filipino students, they are actually considerably more critical of authority. These comparisons, based on comparable samples of older adolescents, are shown in Table 1.

On the face of it, this is strong evidence that the youthful American's investiture of civic and political authority with the qualities of the benevolent leader does not, even in adolescence, prevent a certain autonomy, capacity to criticize, or even disobedience of paternal and political authority. Apparently as the American child grows to maturity, he learns other opinions which counterbalance, to some degree, the earlier *blind* faith and trust in authority. Even so, it is clear that most American children learn from the early grammar school years to trust political authority, to respect it, and to love their country. This positive feeling for political authority, at least, most children share.

The Beginnings of Partisanship

This happy consensus of opinion is disrupted, to some extent, by the fact that these children also begin rather early to identify with certain groups

[3] Edgar Litt, "Civic Education, Community Norms, and Political Indoctrination," *American Sociological Review*, Vol. 28 (1963), p. 73.

[4] Fred I. Greenstein, "The Benevolent Leader: Children's Images of Political Authority," *American Political Science Review*, Vol. 54 (1960), pp. 934–943.

[5] Robert D. Hess and David Easton, "The Child's Changing Image of the President," *Public Opinion Quarterly*, Vol. 24 (1960), pp. 632–644.

[6] See Robert E. Lane, *Political Followership*, forthcoming.

Worse to be a bully than to disobey superiors:

	Yes
Philippine sample	41%
German sample (Bad Homburg)	41
American sample (Oak Park)	85

Right for a soldier to refuse to obey an order to shoot an innocent military prisoner:

	Yes
Philippine sample	66%
German sample	50
American sample	84

Right for a boy to run away from home if father is cruel and brutal:

	Yes
Philippine sample	46%
German sample	45
American sample	80

Should people who unjustly criticize the government of a country be thrown in jail:

	Yes
Philippine sample	31%
German sample	36
American sample	21

Source: Bartlett H. Stoodley, "Normative Attitudes of Filipino Youth Compared with German and American Youth," *American Sociological Review*, Vol. 22 (1957), pp. 557–559.

having conflicting political beliefs—such as religious, ethnic, and racial groups, socio-economic classes, and political parties. Identification with these last two, as we shall see, forms for many purposes the basic touchstones for political partisanship. Let us look first at party identification.

PARTY IDENTIFICATION

Research on youthful political beliefs indicates that children learn to identify with political parties during the grammar school years. For example, Easton and Hess say, about their sample of 700, "A strong majority in each grade from two (age 7–8) through eight (age 13–14) state that if they could vote they would align themselves with (one) of the two major parties in the United States . . . the children may be adopting party identification in much the same way they appropriate the family's religious beliefs, family name, neighborhood location or other basic characteristics of life."[7] Hyman says, "The adult (political) pattern that seems established in most complete form in earlier life is that of *party affiliation.*"[8]

Not only does party preference develop early in life, but it generally follows the preferences expressed by the parents. The dominant trend in

[7] Easton and Hess, "The Child's Political World," *op. cit.*, p. 245.
[8] Herbert Hyman, *Political Socialization* (New York: The Free Press of Glencoe, 1959), p. 46. Hyman's emphasis.

Forming and Weakening the Parental Opinion Tradition

American society seems to be for parents to agree on a party preference, and for the children to adopt that preference. The stability of these early preferences is illustrated by the data from the Survey Research Center's 1952 election survey on adult preferences. As shown in Table 2, this was the dominant trend in their nationwide sample.

Table 2   PARTY PREFERENCE as a Function
of Parental Party Preference

Child's Preference	Both Parents Democrats	Both Parents Republicans	Both Shifted
Democratic	82%	22%	47%
Republican	15	73	37
Other	3	5	16
% of total sample	41	24	6

Source: Angus Campbell, Gerald Gurin, and Warren E. Miller, *The Voter Decides* (New York: Harper, 1954), p. 99.

Clearly if the child's parents agree upon a consistent party preference, the child is extremely likely to adopt that preference. If neither parent can form a consistent preference, the child is much more likely to be independent in his preference. Since the majority of the respondents in this survey had parents who agreed upon a preferred party, and since most of the children followed their parents' choice, it is possible to say that this is the dominant trend in America.

That this transmission of political party loyalties does not occur in all countries, nor even in all Western countries, is illustrated by evidence from Europe. In France most adults do not know what their father's political party or *groupement* was when they were growing up,[9] and in Sweden the age 11–12 group shows 73 per cent "undecided as to best party," the 13–15 group, 66 per cent undecided. Not until age 19 do a majority take the positive party alignment which, in America, was established at age 7 or 8.[10]

We do not have comparable figures on the development of class identification or the use of social class as a guide for political opinions, but there seems to be much more confusion on this point than on party position. For example, among the *high* income group in high schools, the proportion of youth considering themselves members of the working class nearly doubles from 9th to 12th grade (from 14.1 per cent to 25.7 per cent)—a direction which seems the reverse of what one would predict for the relatively better

[9] Philip E. Converse and Georges Dupeux, "Politicization of the Electorate in France and the United States," *Public Opinion Quarterly*, Vol. 26 (1962), pp. 1–23.
[10] Hyman, *op. cit.*, p. 62.

Forming and Weakening the Parental Opinion Tradition

off.[11] On the other hand, this should not be too surprising in view of the fact that even among adults (presumably including these students' parents) there is often a reluctance to make class self-identifications. As many as a third of a nationwide sample were unable or unwilling to identify themselves as members of any social class.[12] Furthermore, in Europe socio-economic classes are more likely to guide political orientations (with alliances between the working class and the socialists and communists, and between the middle class and the more conservative parties), while in the United States party identification is more likely to guide political opinions.[13]

In spite of these confusions on social class, American youth tend to adopt stances on class-related ideological issues fairly early (in the 1940's working-class youth age 16 or younger were twice as "pro-labor" in their issue orientation as middle-class youth at this age level), and these differences increase as they grow older.[14] A concomitant change, partly accounting for this difference, is the increased interest, and the informational support and organization of their ideas: greater organization of opinions is a function of age and education. As a result, by the time adolescents have reached the twelfth grade only 9 to 16 per cent give "undecided" responses to questions on nationalization of railroads, class conflict, the right to strike, and so forth. Their basic political orientations, already fairly firm by the ninth grade, are pretty well settled by the twelfth.[15] And as one might expect, these relatively late advances in interest and orientation occur most often among youth whose family backgrounds gave them the least interest and orientation at the beginning of high school—that is, from homes where the parents were poorest and had the least education.

IMPLICATIONS OF YOUTHFUL PARTISANSHIP

In summary, before the average child reaches high school, he has adopted a partisan attitude toward the two political parties, as well as partisan stances on the major ideological issues. Only a small proportion of students leave high school without some ideological position. These opinions in general are replicas of those held by the child's parents, particularly if the parents agree on the issues and if they express their opinions to the child.

There are two important implications of this dominant pattern. First, if political opinions are in general formed largely as imitations of parental models, clearly a "traditional drag" upon innovation and change will be created. It is important to note, however, that the research on opinion development has focused too narrowly upon party affiliation and candidate preference. It would be highly misleading, for example, to say that no change has ensued between a man's adopting his father's Democratic political preference and voting for Al Smith in 1928, and *his* child's maintaining

11 *Ibid.*, p. 64.
12 See Angus Campbell, Philip E. Converse, Warren E. Miller, and Donald E. Stokes, *The American Voter* (New York: Wiley, 1960), pp. 342–368.
13 Angus Campbell and Henry Valen, "Party Identification in Norway and the United States," *Public Opinion Quarterly,* Vol. 25 (1961), pp. 505–525.
14 Hyman, *op. cit.*, p. 65.
15 *Ibid.*, p. 59.

Forming and Weakening the Parental Opinion Tradition

the familial tradition in voting for John F. Kennedy in 1960. A great many changes in political thinking may have occurred over those two generations, although obscured by the continuity of votes for the Democratic candidate. Hence one of the themes of the subsequent discussion concerns changes in political thinking occurring within what may be a relatively invariant pattern of party preferences.

The second point is that in the course of the development of political consciousness, the child becomes opinionated considerably before he becomes knowledgeable, due largely to imitation of parental preferences in party, candidate, and ideology. The implications of the "lag" in developing knowledgeability will be discussed in Chapter 6.

Before turning to these issues, however, it is necessary to consider the stability of these early, parentally-influenced opinions. Although most children have learned, by the end of adolescence, to parrot their parents' preferences, many influences are at work subsequently to encourage defections from this early learning. Hence it is to the stability of the parental influence that we turn next.

Growing Autonomy: The Impact of School and of Young Adulthood

We have been outlining in a rather sketchy way the childish and adolescent political world; by the time a youth is in high school, this world picture represents, in the first place, the reflection of the parental orientation, second, the effect of maturation processes, including a growing set of capabilities, and third, the influence of the school in developing and changing the politics of the youth in its care. In some ways, then, under these various influences, youth are growing into adults like their parents, and in some ways they are, even as adolescents, departing from the parental pattern. We cannot easily sort out these several influences, but new research has suggested certain ways in which the opinion pattern changes. Among the influences which produce departures from the parental traditions during school years are (a) rebellion against parents and their beliefs, (b) the general educational process, and specifically, civic education in school, and (c) peer-group influence in and out of school, including the prevailing "climate of opinion" among the community of youth. Briefly let us examine these various factors modifying the original political endowment.

REBELLION

The parental model, of course, is so integral a part of many persons that "rebellion" or even deviance may not take place until well into adulthood. Renneker reports the case of a 47-year-old university professor who had "a 'strange' association which flitted across his mind during his father's funeral. He felt a sense of sad relief and was suddenly conscious of the thought that now he could vote for any candidate. This remained puzzling until it was recalled in therapy; it had never occurred to him that he wasn't free to vote

23

for whomever he selected."[16] But our main focus of interest is an adolescent "rebellion," or the rebellion of the young adult still under the influence of his parents.

The minimal extent of this rebellion in party affiliation is suggested by the Survey Research Center data given in Table 2, showing the relationship of parental voting patterns to those of their progeny. Those data indicate that rebellion in party affiliation is relatively infrequent, to say the least. Yet it does happen.

On the whole, the evidence suggests that "political rebellion"—that is, differing from the parents on political matters—when it occurs, has a rather complex set of sources. Middleton and Putney, in a study of 1,440 college students, show that generalized adolescent rebellion (defined by such questions as, "When you were in high school, how often did you defy your parents and do things contrary to their instructions or wishes?") bore little relationship to political rebellion of this particular kind (at least this was true of college students, who are generally of a relatively high socio-economic level).

Nor, for this group, was strictness of parental discipline very important in directly causing political rebellion, but there was a curious roundabout relationship, which was important. Over-strict discipline or over-lenient discipline (probably indifference) tended to reduce the closeness of relationship between child and parents. Then—and this is the important point —the less close a person felt toward his parents, the more likely he was to rebel politically.[17] Here, Middleton's and Putney's work is supplemented by a study by Maccoby, Matthews, and Morton showing that those people in the *lower* socio-economic groups who felt they had suffered from over-strict discipline from their parents *are* likely to rebel politically.[18] Over-strict discipline, then, and to some extent lack of discipline, are, in one way or another, likely to encourage both upper- and lower-class youth to take on political opinions different from those of their parents. Moreover, both studies find that this political rebellion is greater when the parents are interested in politics than when they are not. If they are not interested, as Lane suggested on the basis of his study of working-class father-son relationships, there is not much point in political rebellion. Rather, this study suggests, the political outcome of damaged father-son relationships is apathy and despair over the future of the political order.[19]

It is important to point out, moreover, that rebellion goes in both political directions: the child of a conservative will, under these circumstances, become more radical, and the "rebelling" child of a liberal Democrat becomes more conservative. Rebellion and radicalism have no particu-

[16] Richard E. Renneker, "Some Psychodynamic Aspects of Voting Behavior," in Eugene Burdick and Arthur J. Brodbeck, *American Voting Behavior* (New York: The Free Press of Glencoe, 1959), p. 402.

[17] Russell Middleton and Snell Putney, "Political Expression of Adolescent Rebellion," *American Journal of Sociology,* Vol. 68 (1963), pp. 527–535.

[18] Eleanor E. Maccoby, Richard E. Matthews, and Anton S. Morton, "Youth and Political Change," *Public Opinion Quarterly,* Vol. 18 (1954), pp. 23–29.

[19] Robert E. Lane, "Fathers and Sons: Foundations of Political Belief," *American Sociological Review,* Vol. 24 (1959), pp. 502–511.

Forming and Weakening the Parental Opinion Tradition

lar affinity in this country. And, too, it should be noted that here rebellion is a rather mild differentiation, not an adoption of violent change.

In summary, rebellion against parental beliefs does not play a large role in determining the political opinions of American voters. Under special circumstances, some rebellion does occur, however. It does not have a unidirectional effect; in America, radical ideologies are not the inevitable effect of rebellion against the parents. Finally, it is clear that political rebellion is not an integral part of that constellation we think of as "adolescent rebellion." The rebelling adolescent is much more likely to rebel in terms which are more important to his parents, such as in his dress, his driving, his drinking, his obedience of the law, his sexual behavior, and so forth. Only in rather rare instances does it have political effects as well.

EDUCATION

In an obvious sense, education helps young people to achieve opinions which are different from those of their parents if the parents had less education. But even if the parents had "as much" education it was certainly a different variety since it would be marked by the needs and ideas of a period some twenty-five years earlier. In either event an education helps provide the informational basis and variety of views which make deviance possible. In one sense children are like the people of traditional societies—they have the beliefs and prejudices of a single culture, passed on from father to son. Education modifies this. A study by Pressey illuminates how the changes in the moral and religious norms of society altered the ideas of *college* students over the 1923–1943 period, but did not alter the ideas of high school students.[20] The home and, to some extent, early formal education, encapsulate the past; higher education subjects it to scrutiny in the light of different ideas. Thus, if a young person is ready, for whatever reason, to change from the parental model, school and especially college, facilitate this.

A study of young adults in Cambridge, Massachusetts, reveals these factors in operation at each educational level—though, again, focusing too narrowly on party affiliation and candidate preference (the components of what is called in this study "the Index of Political Change"). The results of this study on education and political change are reported in Table 3. These data show that the degree of change, or deviation from parental beliefs, increases, with only one exception, as the amount of education increases. This is the main point we are making here. There is no reliable trend toward one party or the other as education increases.[21]

[20] S. Pressey, "Changes from 1923 to 1943 in the Attitudes of Public School and University Students," *Journal of Psychology*, Vol. 21 (1946), pp. 173–188.

[21] Maccoby and associates, *op. cit.*, pp. 36–39. There is some reason to view with caution this association of education with a tendency toward political change. National figures do not show a marked discrepancy between the rate of defection among college trained adults compared with others. On the other hand, almost all studies examining ideological change report the marked effect of college education. Probably the association is as indicated, but varies more with the historical period under review than the Maccoby and associates study suggests.

Index of Political Change	College Graduates	Some College	High School plus Business or Vocational	High School Graduates	Some High School
More Republican than parents	24%	32%	17%	27%	23%
No change	42	52	61	58	72
More Democratic than parents	34	16	22	15	5
Total	100%	100%	100%	100%	100%
Number of subjects	55	25	41	88	75

Source: Eleanor E. Maccoby, Richard E. Matthews, and Anton S. Morton, "Youth and Political Change," Public Opinion Quarterly, Vol. 18 (1954), p. 37.

As well as increasing deviation from parental beliefs, the general effect of education is to increase a person's tolerance of heterodoxy, support of civil liberties and civil rights, to reduce his authoritarianism and prejudice, to increase his sense of political effectiveness and rates of participation, and generally to shape a political being who corresponds more closely to the model of the liberal, democratic, informed participant. In every case, however, these attitudes are jointly the product of home and school: students from poorer homes and poorer neighborhoods are less adequate in these respects than those in the equivalent grade from better homes and neighborhoods.

What happens when the school makes a deliberate effort to provide civic and political education for a democratic society? That is, what happens when the school gives special attention to these very goals? In an ingenious study of these programs in three schools serving different socioeconomic groups, Edgar Litt examined the effects of civic education programs upon the political attitudes of adolescent high school students. He focused on four sets of attitudes: (a) elements of the democratic creed ("Every citizen should have an equal chance to influence governmental policy," etc.); (b) political chauvinism ("The American political system is a model that foreigners would do well to copy," etc.); (c) political activity ("It is not very important to vote in local elections," etc.); (d) understanding the political process as conflict adjustment ("Politics should settle social and other disagreements as its major function," etc.).

On each of these four dimensions, students in the upper-class school showed the highest degree of initial agreement with the attitudes being taught. The students in the lower-class school showed the least initial agreement, suggesting that the civic education programs might produce the most change in this group. However, the effects were not uniform with respect to attitude dimensions or in the different schools. In all three schools, the civics programs markedly increased support for the democratic creed, and markedly decreased political chauvinism. No matter what the students' backgrounds or the nature of their schools, they became better citizens in these respects. Presumably, if their initial opinions reflected those of their parents, they became different and better citizens than their parents, as well.

However, education on the last two dimensions (attitudes toward political activity and understanding political conflict) was effective only in the upper-class school. In the middle- and lower-class schools, these parts of the program had little effect. This failure may have been due to the parental cynicism about the political process so prevalent in lower-class homes. However, there was also considerable evidence that the teachers were, in effect, telling the lower-status boys and girls to obey political leaders and conform to these leaders' beliefs, rather than encouraging the children to think they themselves could change things by assuming activ political leadership. The Platonic code (only the "guardians" to be educated for leadership) here, in fact, had its modern incarnation.[22]

PEER-GROUP INFLUENCE AND SCHOOL CLIMATE OF OPINION

One thing that happens to a child as he grows up is that he talks to more people outside his immediate family. The data from some 2,500 high school students in New Jersey, shown in Table 4, indicate that a considerable increase in the discussion of politics with friends occurs during the high school years, although discussion within the family also increases somewhat during this period. The possibility of conflict with parental beliefs thus increases as the child grows older, since his friends may well not hold the same opinions as his parents. For those who are looking for an alternative to family norms and opinions, the peer group may be a potent source of influence.

Table 4   RELATIONSHIP OF AGE TO PARTNERS IN POLITICAL DISCUSSION[a]

Partner in Political Discussion	9th and 10th Grades (1952)	11th and 12th Grades (1954)	Change
Father	66%	66%	0
Mother	39	46	7%
Friend in own grade	23	42	19%

[a] Percentage of students in each grade reporting political discussion with father, mother, and friend.

Compiled from data in Herbert Hyman, *Political Socialization* (New York: The Free Press of Glencoe, 1959), p. 101.

The peer group, however, is only a part of the school community, and the school only part of a wider community. A recent study of the schools teaching some of the same students reported in Table 4 showed that the "climate of opinion" in the schools themselves made a difference. This

[22] Litt, *op. cit.*

Forming and Weakening the Parental Opinion Tradition

climate did not refer to anything the teachers did in the classroom, but rather to the relative proportions of students from Republican and from Democratic families. The rates of defection from parental political opinions were higher for a Democrat in a school with more Republicans, than for a Republican in such a school, and vice versa. Moreover this was more true of boys than girls, probably because they discuss politics more, and because the relative strength of attachments to peer groups and family groups favored the peer groups for these males seeking adolescent independence.[23] Berelson and others refer to this community influence as the "breakage effect"—an analogy from a gambling situation where "the house" wins in a tied conflict. Here the idea is that the community is like "the house" and a community majority will pick up the "votes" or loyalties of people who are conflicted in their opinions. These people will yield their opinions to the majority view.[24] Thus peer groups as friends, and as a community of associates, help, during youth—and, of course, adulthood—to wean a person from the opinions on which his parents nurtured him.

Defections during Adulthood

In an "open society" such as our own, with great geographical and vocational fluidity, the family soon ceases to have the importance in an American's life that it does in more static societies. When the child leaves high school or college, he ordinarily leaves the household of his parents, and often leaves the vicinity altogether. Most young men do not pursue the vocation of their fathers. With decreasing contact with the social environment of his childhood, then, the young adult is subjected to new kinds of influences as he carves out his own niche in society. Often he moves into a distinctively different group of vocational associates; he may marry someone from a background quite dissimilar from his own; his friends and acquaintances may have a political orientation quite different from that held by his friends in his boyhood community. Some of these movements in early adulthood are predominantly in one direction, such as the general movement from rural to urban areas, the emigration of Negroes from the South to industrial areas of the North, and so forth. But others represent an exchange of persons, a two-way movement, with more complicated political consequences.

SOCIAL MOBILITY

Perhaps the most notable example is social mobility, or moving into a social class different from that of one's parents. The socially mobile young adult might well be tempted to become an Independent, as a way of avoiding the conflict between parental beliefs and the predominant political opinions of

[23] Martin L. Levin, "Social Climates and Political Socialization," *Public Opinion Quarterly*, Vol. 25 (1961), pp. 596–606.

[24] Bernard R. Berelson, Paul F. Lazarsfeld, and William N. McPhee, *Voting* (Chicago: University of Chicago Press, 1954), p. 100.

Forming and Weakening the Parental Opinion Tradition

his new social environment. Apparently this does not occur to any great extent. What does happen is rather interesting.

According to Maccoby, Matthews, and Morton, young adults who move up in the social scale adopt the political party of the new, higher class to which they aspire (usually the Republican party), but often retain the lower-class ideology, at least temporarily. On the other hand, those who move down tend to retain the Republican party identification of the middle class, but tend to accept much of the social welfare ideology of the working class.[25] Thus, either kind of mobility creates an inconsistency between ideology and party label—a circumstance which probably makes their political choices less certain for a number of years. Thus the parental tradition persists, in one form or another, into the new situation and creates conflicts with the new belief patterns which emerge in these mobile situations.

Part of the conflict is due to the fact that the young adult is often a kind of marginal man, having firm contacts both with the parental order he is leaving behind and the new circumstances of the life he is moving into. The young adult also frequently lives among friends and co-workers who have not themselves established their life patterns.

However, the stability and homogeneity of one's social environment increases as one grows older; one's friends come to resemble one another (and oneself) more and more closely. In their Elmira sample, for example, Berelson and associates found the following relationship between age and the political agreement of one's three best friends:

Table 5   AGE AND POLITICAL AGREEMENT OF FRIENDSHIP GROUPS

Age	Percentage of Three Best Friends Who Vote the Same as Respondent
21–25	53%
26–34	69
35–44	75
over 45	77

Source: Bernard R. Berelson, Paul F. Lazarsfeld, and William N. McPhee, Voting (Chicago: University of Chicago Press, 1954), p. 97.

The instability and conflict of the young adult's life seems to diminish sharply in his late twenties; there is a rather marked increase in deviation from parental political norms at that point,[26] and, as may be seen in Table 5, a settling down into a homogeneous opinion environment which does not change greatly after that.

MARRIAGES

When a young person marries he (or she) creates a small group which fuses different parental traditions and moves on to create a new order. In

[25] Maccoby and associates, op. cit., pp. 33–36.
[26] Berelson and associates, op. cit., p. 89.

29

general, women tend to leave the political tradition of their parents and to join in the tradition of their husbands: the wife-husband tendency to agree is greater than any other adult family pair. Where this has meant "conversion" it has been preceded by intense political discussion in the home—greater than any discussion among friends or co-workers.[27] If this should fail and a divided family persist, then it appears that the progeny will either tend to be apathetic or some one of the many varieties of independents.

AGING

There is considerable lore on the effect of aging on political ideas, most of it suggesting the increasing conservatism of the older generations. In order to test this hypothesis Crittendon reviewed the American Institute of Public Opinion poll for the 1946 to 1959 period, and analyzed the change of opinion of a series of four year "generations," of which the oldest was a group born between 1878 and 1881, and the youngest was a group born between 1934 and 1937. By comparing the shifts of each of these "generations" to the shifts of all the others he was able to show conclusively that, at least during this historical period, there was a tendency for an increased Republicanism with age, relative to the trend for the entire nation to become more Democratic.[28] Up to the point of retirement older people are usually better off—no doubt that had something to do with it. But for other reasons it is probably also true that older people are less ready for change; that is, they are more conservative. It seems to be established that the longer one associates with a party, or a union, the more intensely loyal one is. Perhaps the same is true of a social order, a set of customs, a cultural pattern—the more one has lived in it, the more one wants it to continue as one has known it over the years.

Historical Change

This discussion has suggested a kind of traditional "drag" on historical change which a variety of forces must overcome. The child tends to accept the beliefs of his parents, and the aging citizen tends to become more conservative. It is the period between childhood and advanced age that provides the opportunities for innovation and change. When the child leaves the parental fold and first discovers, among his classmates and his teachers, that not everyone agrees with his parents, defections can occur. Similarly, when the adolescent takes his first job or goes to college, more of the strands binding him to his childhood are broken, and competing influences can move into the partial vacuum. In young adulthood, the individual gradually forms once again a uniformity of social environment, which in its later stability and homogeneity comes to resemble the social environment of his childhood. However, the political content of this new environment is not the same; the individual has helped to shape his own personal "society"

[27] Maccoby and associates, op. cit., p. 33.
[28] John Crittenden, "Aging and Party Affiliation," Public Opinion Quarterly, Vol. 26 (1962), pp. 648–657.

Forming and Weakening the Parental Opinion Tradition

which, in turn, supports political opinions different from those of his parents.

An interesting example of this has been provided by Newcomb. In the late 1930's he investigated changes in political opinions among girls attending Bennington College. The College itself had only recently opened, with a faculty characterized by liberal political opinions and a high degree of concern about public affairs. Newcomb found that the students, most of whom came from relatively wealthy and conservative families, tended over the duration of their college experience to move toward the liberal norms represented by Bennington. Most of the students had entered the college with conservative political opinions, and their opinions were substantially more liberal four years later.[29]

In a follow-up study conducted in the early 1960's, Newcomb found that the students had, by and large, retained these opinion changes. By then, most of the former students were in a stratum of the population which is generally strongly Republican. Three-quarters were Protestant, and 77 per cent of those who were, or had been, married had annual incomes of $20,000 or more. Yet, 60 per cent had voted for John F. Kennedy, the Democratic candidate, in the 1960 presidential election. Furthermore, 61 per cent approved of admitting Red China to the United Nations, and 76 per cent approved of medical care for the aged under social security—indicating substantial support of bellweather "liberal" positions on highly controversial issues. In contrast, researchers at the Survey Research Center have estimated that in the country as a whole, somewhat less than 25 per cent of the Protestant women college graduates at this income level preferred Mr. Kennedy. The general trend away from conservative opinions which had occurred during the college years, therefore, was largely maintained some two decades later.

A major reason for the persistence of these opinion changes, apparently, was that the women had solicited supportive social environments in the ensuing years. For example, they had married men with educational attainments and social status comparable to their own. However, choice of a mate within this rather rarified, and usually conservative, stratum of society was highly selective. Only 38 per cent of their husbands fell into the normally conservative occupational categories of "management" and "business" (26 per cent preferring Mr. Kennedy), and most of the others were in the more liberally oriented categories of "public employment" and "the professions" (68 per cent preferring Mr. Kennedy). Newcomb argues convincingly, therefore, that the social environment selected by the women after leaving college made an important contribution to the persistence of their changes in opinion. In most cases, the women appeared to have selected an environment which supported the opinions with which they emerged from college.[30]

[29] T. M. Newcomb, *Personality and Social Change* (New York: Dryden, 1943).

[30] T. M. Newcomb, "Interdependence of Attitudes and Environment: Long-Range Studies," 1962 Kurt Lewin Memorial Award Address, delivered at the 1963 annual convention of the American Psychological Association, Philadelphia, September 2, 1963.

Forming and Weakening the Parental Opinion Tradition

Although the ordinary citizen is not exposed to influences which quite so radically overturn their childhood beliefs, we might propose that the pattern is not an uncommon one. If the childhood pattern of influences is broken during the school and young adult years, the subsequent adult environment frequently will be formed in such a way as to support and stabilize the resulting changes of opinion. Furthermore, in this way historical changes can be made. The social environment that John F. Kennedy encountered after he returned from World War II, and the pattern of social influences he was exposed to, were sharply different in some crucial respects from the political environment of his childhood, dominated as it was by his father, Joseph P. Kennedy. By 1963, it was apparent that President Kennedy's political beliefs represented a considerably more modern version of the basic economic liberalism he had grown up with in the 1930's than do the most recent versions of his father's thinking.

Thus it would be a mistake to leave the impression that public opinion is incapable of responding to changing needs and situations. After all, the nation moved from isolationism to internationalism in less than a generation; data which will be presented later reveal a marked shift in attitude toward racial integration; many of those who most hated the New Deal have altered their views after experience with some of its provisions.[31] Much of this, of course, is a general change in which fathers and sons, quite independently, come to a new formulation very different from the one which might have been discussed in their common home a generation ago. But in this change, the son will move faster than his father and more slowly than his own adult son.

[31] Robert E. Lane, *The Regulation of Businessmen* (New Haven: Yale University Press, 1954).

Forming and Weakening the Parental Opinion Tradition

Group
Influence

As is well known, opinions are influenced by group memberships
and group references. How is this done? As we saw
in Chapter 3, individuals absorb from their families
a variety of opinions and values which are later variously supported,
modified, or even "repealed" by the influence of other groups—
for example, peer groups, working cohorts, and the new community
into which a person may move. The influence of a group
in modifying a person's opinions may occur
in any one of several ways. The most apparent are

these: (1) direct personal communication and influence by the members of a group; (2) mass persuasion by a member of a group, such as a union leader addressing a union meeting, or the President of the American Medical Association addressing its members at a national convention; and (3) providing *reference points* which help an individual form his own opinions. For example, when the Democrats and Republicans each announce positions on a new measure, their followers may use these positions (the groups' *norms*) as cues to guide their own opinion formation, even in the absence of any direct attempts at persuasion.

While the first two processes of influence cited above require no additional comment, the third requires further definition. When a group's norms serve as reference points for an individual, the group may be described as one of his *reference groups*. A reference group may be positive, with the individual adopting its norms as his own opinions; or negative, with its norms telling him what *not* to think. The AFL-CIO is of course a positive reference group for many union members, and a negative reference group for numerous businessmen. Clearly, a person does not have to be a member of a group for it to serve a reference function for him.

The rather gross differences among these three processes of influence suggest some distinctions between types of groups. Face-to-face groups are generally called *primary* groups, and generally rely upon face-to-face personal influence. The family group, or a group of workers in an office, or the local chapter of a national fraternity are usually primary groups. Associations, where the relationship between individual and group is rarely personal and intimate, are generally called *secondary* groups. The AFL-CIO, American Medical Association, Democratic party, and NAACP are some of the most politically oriented secondary groups. Finally, there are groups which have no organization but are merely categories, such as age groups, communities, regions, nations, social classes, or the divisions of the population made up of men or of women. These may be termed *categoric* or *tertiary* groups.

Primary-Group Influence

First, it might be well to establish the premise of this discussion. Is it true that face-to-face groups influence an individual's opinion? Is there any pressure to conform to group opinion?

The evidence is substantial in a wide variety of circumstances and on a wide variety of issues. Some of the research has been done on simple perceptual tasks. For example, Sherif has shown that in situations of ambiguous perception (the illusory movement of a point of light), people quickly pick up a group standard and make it their own.[1] Asch has shown that people will violate the clear evidence of their senses to comply with a group which unanimously insists that the longer of two objects is really

[1] Muzafer Sherif, *The Psychology of Social Norms* (New York: Harper, 1936).

shorter.[2] Finally, Bovard has shown that the statement of a leader is often less influential than the group opinion in changing members' opinions.[3]

Small groups are also influential on issues which are of principal concern only to group members. For example, Festinger, Schacter, and Back have shown that in a housing development, those who lived physically closest to others (and their informal conversational networks) were most likely to share the dominant group opinions; the isolates were more likely to be deviants.[4] Merton and Kitt have shown how "green" troops taken as replacements in a veteran outfit quickly adopt the opinions of the veterans, whereas they do not adopt these opinions when placed in all-"green" outfits.[5]

Finally, small groups have also been demonstrably influential in determining the political opinions of their members. We have already mentioned the substantial influence of the family upon children's political opinions. In addition, Gorden has shown that when private opinions on Russia (ascertained before public announcement) are compared with opinions revealed in a public group statement, relatively few maintain publicly the opinions they stated privately: about half move toward the group norm, while a smaller antagonistic group moves away from the group norm.[6] Newcomb has shown that girls who wish to "succeed" in a liberal college, reject their parents' conservative views in favor of the popular dominant liberal views on the campus.[7]

If it is so evident that small groups have such a powerful persuasion effect, how do they do it? What factors influence this process? A variety of studies have shown or suggested the following factors at work. (The starred findings are reported at greater length below.)[8]

Group characteristics

Size: the smaller the group, the stronger the pressure to conform.
Frequency of contact: the more the members of a group interact, the stronger the pressure to conform.
Time: the longer the period during which members of a group have known each other and worked together, the stronger the pressure to conform.

[2] S. E. Asch, "Effects of Group Pressure upon the Modification and Distortion of Judgments," in Dorwin Cartwright and Alvin Zander (eds.), Group Dynamics (Evanston, Ill.: Row, Peterson, 1953), pp. 151–162.

[3] Everett W. Bovard, Jr., "Group Structure and Perception," Journal of Abnormal and Social Psychology, Vol. 46 (1951), pp. 398–405.

[4] L. Festinger, S. Schacter, and K. Back, Social Pressures in Informal Groups (New York: Harper, 1950).

[5] Robert Merton and Alice S. Kitt, "Contributions to the Theory of Reference Group Behavior," in Merton and Paul F. Lazarsfeld (eds.), "The American Soldier," Continuities in Social Research (New York: The Free Press of Glencoe, 1950), pp. 40–105.

[6] Raymond L. Gorden, "Interaction Between Attitude and the Definition of the Situation in the Expression of Opinion," American Sociological Review, Vol. 17 (1952), pp. 50–58.

[7] Theodore M. Newcomb, Personality and Social Change (New York: Dryden, 1943).

[8] Some of the studies on which the following generalizations are based are indexed and summarized in Paul Hare, Edgar F. Borgatta, and Robert F. Bales (eds.), Small Groups: Studies in Social Interaction (New York: Knopf, 1955).

Participation in decisions: the more individuals participate in making decisions, the more likely they are to accept these decisions.

Group-centeredness: group-centered groups compared with leader-centered groups exert stronger pressures to conform.

Cohesiveness (sense of solidarity, feeling of "we-ness"): the higher the cohesiveness of the group, the stronger the pressure to conform.

Group salience: the more salient the basis for group membership in a given context, the greater the pressure to conform.

Clarity of group norm: the less ambiguous the appropriate group norm, the greater the pressure to conform (and ease of conforming).

Homogeneity: the more homogeneous the membership opinion on a given issue, the greater the pressure to conform on that issue.

Issues

*Group relevance: the more related the issue to the purpose of the group, the stronger the pressures to conform to group opinion on that issue.

Ambiguity: the more ambiguous the issue and the less relevant the experiential standards of an individual, the greater the pressure to conform.

Individual characteristics

*Feelings of acceptance: members with average, as contrasted with high or low acceptance in the group, are more susceptible to pressures to conform.

Affiliative needs: the more an individual feels the need for acceptance by the group (or perhaps by others generally) the more susceptible he is to group induction.

Group purpose and individual purpose: the more the purposes and goals of the group are congruent with the purposes and goals of the individual, the more he feels the pressure to conform.

Instrumentality: the more the group serves as an instrument for individual goals (advancement, prestige, "contacts"), the more an individual experiences the pressures to conform.

*Personality: weaker egos, stronger capacities for group loyalties, other-directedness, lower self-esteem, timidity in intergroup relations, lack of hostility, and other personal factors contribute to greater willingness or need to conform to group standards.

Setting

Group status: the higher the status of the group, the stronger the pressure to conform.

External opposition: the greater the perception of external threat to the group, the greater the pressure to conform.

Alternative groups: the fewer the alternative groups available to meet similar needs, the stronger the pressures to conform.

Many of these relationships are obvious; some are different from what might be expected; a few are contested by different experiments (but the weight lies currently with the relationship indicated); some seem to "work" only in combinations with others. As findings, they come to life, and their implications are more clearly seen, when the research which supports them is portrayed, however briefly. Here we set forth three of the studies behind these conclusions and draw a few broader implications from their findings.

    Group relevant issues. In several studies it has been shown that the pressures to conform are greater on an issue which is directly relevant to the goals and purposes of the group than on other kinds of issues. For example, Schacter set up movie and radio clubs to serve a market research function, purportedly for the local theater owners and the local radio station, and case-study clubs were set up to evaluate the case of a juvenile delinquent for a group of lawyers, judges, and social workers. All clubs were given the juvenile delinquency case-study to work on, which means that the actual discussion was highly relevant to the purpose of the case-study clubs, and largely irrelevant for the movie and radio clubs. For the case-study clubs the discussion was more concentrated and less superficial.[9]

This finding, and others like it, is not in itself surprising; but it does help us to understand some of the characteristics of American public opinion. For one thing, it suggests why people's opinions tend to be fragmented and compartmentalized—different opinions are anchored in different and rather narrowly specialized groups. Furthermore, it helps to explain why associations have trouble developing larger ideological constructs to rationalize their specific aims (compared with European politics, in which rationalization of this kind is more common). They do not do this because their clienteles lose interest when organization leaders move beyond the specific group-relevant issue before them. Of course, the Schacter study does not prove this—but it is suggestive.

Group acceptance. Acceptance of individual members by the group might make the group norms more attractive and increase the pressures to conform, or, alternatively, acceptance might give a person a kind of security and "freedom" to be different. Dittes and Kelley experimentally varied the extent to which the group as a whole accepted each of the members. The group carried out a task, then each member evaluated the other members with respect to who should be continued as members and who should not. The experimenter substituted four kinds of ratings for the genuine ratings, producing four levels of acceptance: higher than average acceptance, average acceptance, slightly below average, and well below average. The groups were then given problems to work out in which the amount of opinion changes toward the group norm could be measured.

The findings generally showed that the *average* acceptance subjects, those who were accepted as members of the group but who could possibly increase their degree of acceptance, tended to conform the most. They also reacted to information discrepant from the group norm with the greatest speed, and participated most in the group discussion. In other words, those with potential for upward mobility in the group were most conformist and most eager to dispute information which ran counter to the group norms. On the other hand, those who were above average in acceptance, in some sense a secure elite within the group, conformed least to the group norms. But they also tended to value membership in the group most.[10]

[9] S. Schacter, "Deviation, Rejection, and Communication," *Journal of Abnormal and Social Psychology,* Vol. 46 (1951), pp. 190–207.

[10] J. Dittes and H. H. Kelley, "Effects of Different Conditions of Acceptance upon Conformity to Group Norms," *Journal of Abnormal and Social Psychology,* Vol. 53 (1956), pp. 629–36.

For the moment, it is this sense of security in the group which attracts our attention. If it is true, indeed, that a feeling of high acceptance and security in a group frees a man to run counter to the group norms, these secure elites are somewhat freer to work for compromise and adjustment to the demands of other groups. From other studies we know that community leaders are, indeed, more tolerant of several kinds of heterodoxy than are the rank and file of community members.[11] The small group findings and the community leaders findings reinforce each other, and, at the same time frame a question for a pluralistic democracy: If people with only average acceptance and no official status in a group are least flexible, *how much control by rank and file members of groups do we want?*

Individual variety and individualized "group conflict." We suggested above a variety of personality factors which affect susceptibility to the pressures to conform (self-esteem, timidity, capacities for group loyalties, and so forth). As mentioned earlier, Gorden surveyed the members of a housing cooperative on their opinions on Russia. He first got their opinions in private, then forced them to state their opinions in a group situation where all might hear them and to estimate the nature of the group opinion. He found that 54 per cent of the group shifted their opinions toward the group norm, 33 per cent shifted away from the group norm, and 12 per cent retained in public the same opinions they had expressed in private. Then comparing extreme conformists and extreme nonconformists (those moving from the group norm) he found first that the conformists were characterized by personal factors making group acceptance especially important for them, leading them to undervalue the importance of expressing a "true" opinion compared with winning group approval. On the other hand the nonconformists had personality factors which made them positively value the opposition of the group. Second, while the conformists tended to believe that if they deviated from the group opinion they might lose their status or group acceptance, the nonconformists defined the situation of the deviant in a very different and much less threatening fashion.[12]

Compared with that of other countries American social conflict tends to be *individualized* rather than collectivized, although there are many exceptions. This is the product of a variety of social situations, especially multiple-group memberships, but one contribution to this pattern is the very tendency of people to respond to group pressures in different ways, which Gorden has analyzed. As we shall see, the atomization of conflict, as in France, is often not a healthy thing, but at least it tends to prevent polarized inter-group conflict.

The relevance of these small-group processes to the formation of public opinion is increased when it is related to another major force in opinion formation, the mass media. The relationship is suggested in the idea of a "two-step flow," that is, the idea that the messages in the media reach their "targets," not only through direct exposure, but through the "retailing" of

[11] Samuel A. Stouffer, *Communism, Conformity, and Civil Liberties* (Garden City, N.Y.: Doubleday, 1955).
[12] Gorden, *op. cit.*

Group Influence

these messages by certain "opinion leaders" talking to their friends, co-workers, relatives, parent-teacher associations, lodge chapters, union locals, and other primary groups. That there is this personal chain of communications both during and between campaign periods has been well established by several studies.[13] In general these opinion leaders tend to be slightly better educated and have slightly higher status than their "audiences," a factor which gives them a little more authority in small-group discussions. These leaders have access to others who are, in turn, slightly "higher" than they are in the social structure. This might be thought to introduce a conservative effect on public opinion, but the evidence is not at all clear-cut on this point.

Reference Groups

The quality that is special to primary-group relationships is the influence of face-to-face relationships. It is a matter of people dealing directly with other people. The quality that is central to reference groups (which are often secondary or tertiary groups, with little personal contact) is the nature and manner of identification of the person with the group. Let us, then, briefly explore some kinds of identifications (and disidentifications) and learning processes involved in reference-group behavior.

In the first place, the evidence for the influence of group identification upon opinions and beliefs is almost as strong for secondary groups as it is for primary groups. Indeed some of the evidence cited above shows the impact of both groups: The college girls who identified with the liberal college group rather than with their own families tended to adopt the liberal college norms more quickly. The replacement soldiers who identified with their new units tended to adopt the veterans' views more quickly than did those who failed to make this identification. But more specifically, even in the absence of personal contact and induction, the reference group does its work.

Eulau has shown that people who think of themselves as middle class tend to take on the political views of the middle class, even though they are immersed in a working-class milieu.[14]

Campbell and his associates have shown that those for whom membership in a particular group (e.g., labor union, ethnic or religious group) is most significant, tend, more than those otherwise like themselves, to adopt the attitudes and political opinions of that group.[15]

Freeman and Showel have shown that people openly select for political guidance and reference associations of which they are members or

[13] See Elihu Katz and Paul F. Lazarsfeld, *Personal Influence* (New York: The Free Press of Glencoe, 1955); Bernard R. Berelson, Paul F. Lazarsfeld, and William N. McPhee, *Voting* (Chicago: University of Chicago Press, 1954), pp. 109–114.

[14] Heinz Eulau, *Class and Party in the Eisenhower Years* (New York: The Free Press of Glencoe, 1962).

[15] Angus Campbell, Philip E. Converse, Warren E. Miller, and Donald E. Stokes, *The American Voter* (New York: Wiley, 1960), p. 309.

would like to be members (plus—an interesting exception—neutral groups that seem to rise above the conflict).[16]

The evidence is clear that reference groups are highly significant in molding opinions. Indeed, it has even been said that when a person has "no opinion," it is for one of just three reasons: (1) the individual has no reference group within which a stand is taken relevant to the proposition; (2) he cannot shift psychologically to the right reference group, perhaps because he has conflicting references; or (3) he is unaware of the stand which his appropriate group has taken or would take if asked.[17]

Reference groups help people achieve a life perspective. The kinds of opinions and identifications we have been considering have been somewhat segmental, often rather ephemeral, and not always close to the center of men's attention and concern. But group references and group identifications go deeper than that; they provide the material for the deepest beliefs and emotions that people can have. One of these has to do with a person's view of his *life space*, the social and geographical area in which he will find his friends, his audience. "Life space" refers to the people whose approval he seeks or whose disapproval he fears, those with whom he is in competition as well as those with whom he can relax and play. In this sense, a positive reference group is a group with whom a person shares a common destiny and therefore one whose fortunes he will seek to improve and for whom he is willing to make demands. It is, in Lewin's phrase, the "social ground" on which he stands.[18]

Moreover, a person's reference groups are the source of his *social identity*, that is, part of his answer to the question, "Who am I?" A person defines himself, in part, by the groups he belongs to: "I am a Texan, a 32nd degree Mason, a Baptist, and an American." From this definition he derives a set of cues which tell him how to behave, tell what are the appropriate values and goals and codes for "a person in my position." If, as it happens, he achieves an identity which is reinforced by his environment— the world tells him that he "is" what he thinks he "is"—he has a secure basis for going forth and meeting others and doing his share of the world's work in peace. If, through error, he achieves a false identity—a choice which is not congruent with what others think of him—he is in trouble.[19]

A person's reference groups will also give a *picture of reality and a way of "knowing" it*, in philosophical terms, a metaphysics and an epistemology. Among other things, these groups will provide for him a time schedule which will help him to interpret the stream of historical events of which, in some small way, he is a part. Kluckhohn and Strodtbeck found that one

[16] Howard E. Freeman and Morris Showel, "Differential Political Influence of Voluntary Associations," *Public Opinion Quarterly*, Vol. 15 (1951–52), pp. 703–714.

[17] Eugene L. Hartley, "The Social Psychology of Opinion Formation," *Public Opinion Quarterly*, Vol. 14 (1950–51), pp. 668–774.

[18] Kurt Lewin, *Resolving Social Conflicts* (New York: Harper, 1948), pp. 169–185.

[19] Erik Erikson, *Childhood and Society* (New York: Norton, 1950), pp. 244–283; Robert E. Lane, *Political Ideology* (New York: The Free Press of Glencoe, 1962), pp. 381–399.

of the principal differences between a Mexican-American community and a Protestant Texan community living only a few miles apart was their sense of the importance of the passage of time, and their interest in the future. The Mexican-Americans were more interested in the present and the past; the Protestant Texans were more interested in the future.[20] Similarly, the boundaries of space as perceived by the individual will be traced by the attention and conversation of the people and groups he associates himself with. Is he parochial? Then it is because his friends and associates are parochial. Is he an internationalist? Is he concerned with a fantasy world defined by television and the comics? It is the rare person who greatly transcends, or greatly limits, the attention boundaries of the people and groups important to him.

It is the same way with the definition of "facts" and the orientation towards the sources of knowledge. What is authoritative knowledge? Obviously, a person is likely to accept as authoritative what others whom he respects consider authoritative. Few people work this out for themselves. Karl Marx thought that men would take their views on society from their social and economic class, once they learned to locate themselves in this way. More generally, now, it appears that Karl Marx's view was much too narrow; men tend to take their broader perspectives on life from their geographical, familial, ethnic, occupational, and "class" positions.[21]

Conflicting group identifications. We have spoken of group references and group identifications as though a person were confronted with a set of isolated choices. But of course each person has many group references, and sometimes these multiple references make conflicting demands. How shall he deal with these conflicts? There is considerable evidence to show that when these conflicts are actually experienced by the individual (and not merely read into their situation by an outside observer), there is a tendency to withdraw from the conflict situation or the painful choice. Elsewhere, Lane has suggested some other responses to such "cross pressures":

> Withdrawal from a decision involving conflicting reference groups is only one of several means of solving the conflict problem; others include (a) identification with one of the conflicting reference groups (sometimes because of frustration in the other), (b) moderation in viewpoint, a moderation which may be either confused and eclectic or synthesized, (c) minimization of the issue, (d) failure to "see" the conflict, (e) generalized apathy (where the conflicting groups embrace large areas of life).[22]

The handling of these problems of conflicting group identifications is part of the individual's general strategy for dealing with multiple loyalties, a strategy guided on the one hand by his unique personality and on the other hand by the customary methods of treating multiple loyalties in his

[20] Florence R. Kluckhohn and Fred L. Strodtbeck, *Variations in Value Orientations* (Evanston, Ill.: Row, Peterson, 1961), pp. 10–20.

[21] See Karl Mannheim, *Ideology and Utopia* (New York: Harcourt, Brace, 1949).

[22] Robert E. Lane, *Political Life: Why People Get Involved in Politics* (New York: The Free Press of Glencoe, 1959), p. 203.

culture. For example, Guetzgow suggests that multiple loyalties develop best among those who have learned first to be loyal to one group; it is a transferable and generalizable trait.[23] On the other hand, the lesson of the study called *The Authoritarian Personality* is that those who develop an intensive loyalty to one in-group, tend often to develop hostilities to all other groups, conceiving of them as strange or hostile or somehow beyond the pale.[24] Partly, of course, people with one personality constellation will reveal the Guetzgow syndrome, those with another personality constellation (authoritarian personalities) will show the authoritarian in-group out-group pattern. But partly, too, it is a matter of social training. In an open, mobile society people are, perforce, taught multiple loyalties; they are encouraged to think of themselves as partisans of many groups, some of which, inevitably conflict. Easton and Hess report that children learn a moderate partisanship early in life:

. . . it is quite revealing to discover that, young as they are, children in the early grades learn to tolerate partisan commitment on their part and to accept alternative partisanship on the part of others as one of the rules of the game. Partisan differences—and at times even conflict—so generated are not interpreted as hampering the acceptance of the outcome of electoral campaigns, esteem for the victor, or the legitimacy of the authority so established. This constitutes the beginning of what later in life becomes a rather complex set of attitudes and represents an introduction to a major norm of democratic society.[25]

To some extent, then, the school and home are teaching children a capacity for multiple loyalties and a tolerance for other people's different loyalties, not a preference for in-group out-group dispositions.

[23] Harold S. Guetzgow, *Multiple Loyalties: Theoretical Approach to a Problem in International Organization* (Princeton, N.J.: Center for Research on World Political Institutions, 1955).

[24] T. W. Adorno, E. Frenkel-Brunswik, D. J. Levinson, and R. N. Sanford, *The Authoritarian Personality* (New York: Harper, 1950), pp. 146–150.

[25] David Easton and Robert E. Hess, "The Child's Political World," *Midwest Journal of Political Science*, Vol. 6 (1962), pp. 244–245.

Leaders'
Influence
On
Public Opinion

A General Approach to Influence

Since the main focus of this little book
is upon "public opinion," our interest centers upon the public
as a whole, rather than upon specialized elites
such as politicians, congressmen, bureaucrats, or any
other selected groups. As an audience for attempts at persuasion,
the public as a whole is for the most part marked
by relatively modest interest in political

43

matters and relatively low levels of information. Furthermore, many of the persuasive attempts which are of interest to us must be carried out at a distance, through messages over television and radio and reports in the press. Occasionally the influence attempt is more personalized: an address by an individual at a lodge meeting or political rally, or personal influence attempts made by local opinion leaders and acquaintances. We turn now to a description of a set of general principles for influence which hold, by and large, for both personal influence and mass communication situations.

In any influence situation, someone (the "source") is attempting to persuade someone else (the "influencee" in the audience) to adopt a given position. Our concern is with the influencee and the circumstances under which he will in fact adopt that position. In a simple influence situation, the influencee has three basic sets of "cognitions" or "thoughts": his *evaluation of the source,* his *judgment of the source's position,* and his own *opinion* on the issue. Let us consider each of these.

Own opinion. We have examined the nature of an opinion in the second chapter. It is a complex matter, comprised of direction and intensity (which will be our main concerns in this chapter), existing in a public-opinion context which makes it normal or extreme, and implying some promise of stability. The effort is sometimes made to change a whole cluster of opinions held by an influencee. This then involves matters of organization, informational base, salience, and policy orientation.

Evaluation of the source of the influence. The specific evaluation rendered by a particular influencee is of interest to us here. Especially, we want to know whether he has a positive or a negative feeling toward the source, and how intense the feeling is. Other pertinent dimensions of evaluation concern the source's trustworthiness, credibility, and expertness.

Judgment of the source's position. The third set of cognitions consists of the influencee's judgment of the position held by the source. This judgment does not always correspond to the position *actually* held by the source, of course. Often members of the audience are motivated to misperceive and misunderstand what a source has said. For example, among Democrats in 1948 who supported the Taft-Hartley Law, 40% thought President Truman also supported it, and 60% thought he opposed it.[1] Actually, of course, he had vetoed it in 1947, and campaigned in 1948 partly on the basis of his opposition.

Considerable research has, in recent years, supported the idea of a "strain toward consistency" among the above three sets of cognitions. In its simplest form this idea merely asserts that people tend to agree with people they like and tend to like people who agree with them. Under these circumstances,

[1] Bernard R. Berelson, Paul F. Lazarsfeld, and William N. McPhee, *Voting* (Chicago: University of Chicago Press, 1954), p. 221.

Leaders' Influence on Public Opinion

the three sets of cognitions are "consonant," or consistent with each other.[2] The reverse of this situation, created by a conflict between a positive evaluation of the source and a negative evaluation of the position he holds (or vice versa—a negative evaluation of the source and a positive evaluation of his position), yields "cognitive dissonance." Dissonance is a state of psychological tension which motivates efforts to restore these cognitions to a "consonant" or consistent state. We shall explore how this is done below. In the meantime, an example may help.

Suppose that the President of your college, whom you like and respect, is reported to have argued that admission of Jews to your college should be limited to 10 per cent of the incoming freshman class—a position with which you disagree. The three elements of the influence situation are present: your own opinion on such a quota system, your favorable evaluation of the President, and your perception of his position. Clearly some tension is involved (and the more important you feel the matter is, and the more intensely you feel about it, the stronger the tension). This tension may be relieved in several obvious ways: perhaps by changing your opinion on the proposed quota system (e.g., "we should have a balanced school body," or "I'll bet that's all the qualified Jews that apply, anyway"), perhaps by changing your evaluation of the President (e.g., "Anyone who would take such a bigoted position as that must be a real SOB"), or perhaps by changing your perception of his position (e.g., "It was only a rumor," or "He must have said that's the proportion that is coming in next year, not that only 10 per cent *should* come."), or perhaps in some other ways to be explored below.

From this simple three-element influence situation, a variety of patterns emerge. An oversimplified but helpful diagram (Table 6) of the vari-

Table 6 INFLUENCE SITUATIONS

	Consonant Situations				Dissonant Situations			
	(1)	(2)	(3)	(4)	(5)	(6)	(7)	(8)
Your evaluation of the source	+	+	−	−	+	+	−	−
Positions on the issue:								
Source's position, as you perceive it	+	−	+	−	+	−	+	−
Your own position	+	−	−	+	−	+	+	−

[2] A number of theorists have developed the general idea of a "strain toward consistency," among them Fritz Heider, "Attitudes and Cognitive Organization," *Journal of Psychology,* Vol. 21 (1946), pp. 107–112; Charles E. Osgood and Percy Tannenbaum, "The Principle of Congruity and the Prediction of Attitude Change," *Psychological Review,* Vol. 62 (1955), pp. 42–55; Leon Festinger, *A Theory of Cognitive Dissonance* (Evanston, Ill.: Row-Peterson, 1957); and Robert P. Abelson and Milton J. Rosenberg, "Symbolic Psycho-Logic: A Model of Attitudinal Cognition," *Behavioral Science,* Vol. 3 (1958), pp. 1–13. The terms we use are those proposed by Festinger, although the present analysis deviates to some degree from his, and borrows from all these writers.

ations in these elements will help to define those four which produce consonance (and no pressure to change any of the elements) as opposed to those four which produce dissonance (and pressure to change one or more of the elements). First, a person may evaluate the source positively or negatively; second, he may perceive the source as supporting or opposing a particular position on the issue; and third, he may himself evaluate that position positively or negatively.

As may be seen in Table 6, if you perceive the source as sharing your position on the issue, dissonance is created only if you evaluate him negatively (because you dislike him, do not respect him, feel he is untrustworthy, etc.). However, if you perceive the source as disagreeing with you on the issue, dissonance is created if you evaluate him positively (because you like him, respect him, trust him, etc.). The above example of your college President is represented in Table 6 by dissonant combination (5). You disagree with him on the quota system, but you have always before thought rather well of him.

THE MAGNITUDE OF DISSONANCE: DISCREPANCY AND IMPORTANCE

In actuality, of course, influence situations are more complicated than implied by these basic paradigms of consonant and dissonant situations, and such complications affect the magnitude of pressure to change. Two such considerations are of particular importance. One is *opinion discrepancy*. Whenever a source, in delivering a communication designed to persuade, endorses some position on the "pro-con" continuum, we may describe the distance between his position on the continuum and the position of the influencee as "opinion discrepancy." It is the discrepancy between the source's position and the influencee's position. Let us imagine two situations to illustrate the effect of discrepancy: one, that former President Eisenhower states that only those with property should be allowed to vote; another, that he states that no elections should be held at all. Both are dissonant, in that a generally popular source is endorsing generally unpopular positions. However, the second produces more dissonance than the first, since his no-election position is more distant from our own position than is his property-requirement position.

It is generally assumed that as discrepancy increases, given positively evaluated sources, dissonance and pressure to conform to source's opinion also increase.[3] In some cases the possibility of opinion change also increases, and in some cases it decreases, as we will see later on. When a negatively evaluated source is involved, dissonance is assumed to decrease with greater discrepancy, since a disliked opinion from a disliked source does not at all create a conflict of attitudes.

A second consideration is the *importance* of the issue to the person. Clearly if the issue, like the minimum wage law or the graduated income

[3] L. Festinger and·E. Aronson, "The Arousal and Reduction of Dissonance in Social Contexts," in D. Cartwright and A. Zander (eds.), *Group Dynamics*, second edition (Evanston, Ill.: Row, Peterson, 1960).

Leaders' Influence on Public Opinion

tax, makes some considerable difference for *that* person's economic welfare, greater dissonance will be aroused than if the issue is trivial or remote to him, such as whether or not an obscure immigrant should be deported.

After the source has aroused dissonance in his listener, his main concern will be with the way in which the person decides to reduce the dissonance. There is a variety of ways to convert a dissonant situation into a consonant one, but the source usually hopes his listener will decide to reduce his dissonance by changing his opinion. The most obvious alternatives to opinion change are reevaluation of the source and distortion of the source's position, but others will be mentioned below.

In general, the influencee will reduce dissonance by changing those cognitions that are "easiest" to change. In the example given earlier, if the President's position on the quota system did indeed reach you only as an incidental and unsubstantiated rumor, it might be easiest merely to assert that he holds the opposite position; i.e., that he actually opposes the quota system. On the other hand, if you heard him make the statement yourself, and you felt very intensely that the quota system was wrong, it might be easiest to derogate the source; i.e., lower your respect for the President.

It may now be seen why the intensity of an opinion is extremely important. If a source with some prestige attempts to change opinions which are very different from his own and which are very strongly held, he is likely only to reduce his prestige. Very intense opinions are not usually the "easiest" cognitions to change. Source derogation rather than opinion change is most likely to be selected as the mode of dissonance-reduction. This was illustrated dramatically by the concerns expressed during President Kennedy's Administration over his loss of popularity in the South. He had, of course, taken a position on civil rights which ran counter to the extraordinarily intense opinions generally held in the South about segregation. By doing so, he appeared to have damaged his prestige (and vote-getting ability) in the South as much as or more than he had changed Southern opinions about segregation.

THE MANY ROADS TO CONSONANCE: MODES OF DISSONANCE-REDUCTION

Opinion change and source reevaluation. If a political leader, such as the Mayor of your city, or former President Eisenhower, or Premier Khrushchev (or a newspaper editor or television commentator, for that matter) seeks to change the attitudes of his audience, he will be confronted with the following general tendencies, by now well-established in experimental research.

For any given message, the better the reputation of the source, the more likely people are to agree with the message. A substantial amount of evidence shows that a message attributed to a credible (positive) source is more likely to be believed than the identical message attributed to a less credible (negative) source.[4] This seems obvious enough, on the face of it.

[4] C. I. Hovland and W. Weiss, "The Influence of Source Credibility on Communication Effectiveness," *Public Opinion Quarterly*, Vol. 15 (1951), pp. 635–650.

Leaders' Influence on Public Opinion

The corollary is that the greater the audience agreement with any given message, the better its estimation of the source.[5] This is, of course, why politicians say popular things; one important way in which a politician builds a "reputation" in the first place is to advocate that which his constituency agrees with. But since these are only tendencies, it is the exception that is interesting: the politician who improves his reputation by saying unpopular things.

Now let us consider somewhat more complicated situations. One question of interest concerns how much change a given source should advocate. For example, will a prominent national figure, such as the President, get more opinion change in the public if he advocates a highly discrepant position, such as the institution of a Federal Fair Employment Practices Commission with compulsory powers, or a less discrepant position, such as the institution of a committee to discuss discriminatory employment on a voluntary basis with employers? The question we are concerned with here is the degree of change advocated, or opinion discrepancy. As we shall see, the answer to the question depends very much both on the prestige of the source and upon the intensity of public feeling on the issue.

The "weakest link" hypothesis stated that the resolution of dissonance would press toward opinion change, source reevaluation, or distortion of the source's position, depending on which cognitions were least intensely held. The discrepancy hypothesis stated that the greater the opinion distance between source and audience, the greater the pressure to change. In the following pair of experiments we see that this *greater pressure to change is translated into greater opinion change only when the opinion is the weakest link;* e.g., when there are strong sources and weak opinions. Conversely, when relatively weak sources attempt to change strong opinions, the reverse holds; that is, the more the discrepancy the less the opinion change, and the greater the source derogation. In both experiments the sources' positions were quite unequivocal, which largely ruled out distortion.

Hovland and Pritzker carried out an experiment in the early 1950's in which the subjects' opinions on the issues were of low intensity.[6] High school students were used, and the issues included such thing as "the number of movie theaters likely still to be open by 1954" and the likelihood of "atomic power electricity by 1954." Evaluation of the sources were probably more intense, however, since the subjects were first asked whether teachers, historians, or parents would be the greatest authorities on the issues used. And later, in fact, those indicated as the greatest authorities were used as the sources of the messages in the study. Under such conditions, it was found that the greater the "opinion discrepancy" between the sources' position and the respondents' positions the *greater* the change.

With strong opinions and weak sources, source derogation should be the preferred mode of resolution. This relationship was graphically illustrated by Hovland, Harvey, and Sherif, who took an issue on which

[5] Osgood and Tannenbaum, *op. cit.*
[6] C. I. Hovland and H. A. Pritzker, "Extent of Opinion Change as a Function of Amount of Change Advocated," *Journal of Abnormal and Social Psychology*, Vol. 54 (1957), pp. 257–261.

Leaders' Influence on Public Opinion

the subjects had very intense opinions then and exposed them to a persuasive communication from an anonymous source. The issue was prohibition, and all the subjects were residents of a "dry" state in which prohibition was a lively source of controversy. The subjects fell into three categories: "drys," strongly favoring prohibition (among them, members of the WCTU and the Salvation Army); "moderates," generally taking a compromise position on the issue; and "wets," strongly opposed to prohibition. In this experiment, the greater the opinion discrepancy between the source's position and the respondents' position, the *less* the opinion change produced. For example, when the source took a "wet" position, he had virtually no success at all with the "drys," nor was he any more effective taking a "dry" position with "wet" subjects. The source was somewhat more effective when he took a position less discrepant from that initially held by the subjects (when he took a "wet" position with "moderate" subjects, or a "moderately wet" position with "dry" subjects, for example).[7]

The results of the two studies are quite opposite, reflecting the differences in intensities of evaluation of opinion and source. In the first study, the greater dissonance produced by the highly discrepant message was presumably reduced by more opinion change. However, the greater dissonance produced by highly discrepant messages in the prohibition study was evidently reduced in quite a different way.

We would expect that dissonance stemming from highly discrepant communications would be reduced by disparaging the source when a weak source tries to change an extremely strong opinion. This was indeed the case; the more the anonymous source's position differed from the highly intense opinions held by the subjects, the less favorably was the communication evaluated, that is, the more the source was derogated.[8]

We may now advise our more or less persuasive mayors, newspapers, and national leaders that:

On any given issue, the greater the change in opinion they advocate, the greater will be the audience change—*if* the audience respects them highly *and* if it has relatively weak convictions on the matter.

But, they should also know:

On any given issue, the greater the change in opinion they advocate, the more they will be criticized and the less change they will get—*if* the audience already has strong opinions on the issue, and is somewhat indifferent to them as advocates.

It is somewhat easier now to see why the fears of a Burke or a de Tocqueville about the power of demagogic leadership in a popularly elected government are exaggerated. Public opinion places considerable restraint upon the ability of a leader successfully to advocate important measures

[7] Carl I. Hovland, O. J. Harvey, and Muzafer Sherif, "Assimilation and Contrast Effects in Reactions to Communication and Attitude Change," *Journal of Abnormal and Social Psychology*, Vol. 55 (1957), pp. 244–252.
[8] *Ibid.*

which do not accord in some degree with public opinion. Even the most prestigious public figures cannot achieve general opinion change in the face of significant opposition. President Roosevelt could not "pack" the Supreme Court, as popular as he was, and Woodrow Wilson was unable to get the United States into the League of Nations, and neither of these issues were as intensely regarded as, for example, segregation. Many an important public figure has fallen from power because he advocated too radical a change, and was instead himself devaluated by the voters.

Distortion of the source's position. We have spoken of changes in two elements in an influence situation: opinions on the issue and evaluations of the source. There remains a third element, and thus a third possible method of dissonance reduction—judgment of the source's position.

Berelson and his colleagues have found that the voter generally perceives greater agreement between his views and his candidate's positions than exists in fact. They also found that voters are more likely to be ignorant of or wrong about *their* candidate's positions if in fact they are in disagreement with the candidate than if in fact they agree with his positions.[9] These findings could, of course, be interpreted in two ways: as distortion or suppression of knowledge of the candidate's position due to the dissonance aroused by the discrepancy, or as a function of ignorance (perhaps if a Democrat had known what Truman's position was on the Taft-Hartley Act, he would have agreed with it).

However, findings about post-election reactions to defeat suggest that distortion, not ignorance, is the main factor here; that is, perceptions of a candidate's positions are actually distorted as a means of reducing dissonance. Thus Sears and Freedman found that after the election of 1960, supporters of Richard M. Nixon were able to improve their evaluation of President-elect Kennedy, not by changing their opinions on campaign issues to conform with his, but by changing their perceptions of Kennedy's positions so that his views conformed more closely to their own. That this was a dissonance-reducing distortion is further indicated by the fact that no such change in perception of Kennedy's position occurred among the triumphant Democrats.[10]

One interesting hypothesis about the *direction* in which a source's position is distorted has been derived from psychophysical studies of assimilation and contrast. When a member of the audience receives a message from someone he respects, and it differs mildly from his own position, he is likely to *assimilate* the position and thus claim it to be very similar to his own. For example, a Southerner might say, "President Eisenhower never spoke out against segregation, despite the pressures on him to do so. That indicates that he basically agrees with me, that integration is wrong." Consonance is thus produced in the form of $+++$, or perhaps $+--$ (as in this example), using the symbols given in Table 6.

On the other hand, when a person receives a message of intermediate

[9] Berelson and associates, *op. cit.*, pp. 220–30.

[10] David O. Sears and J. L. Freedman, "Organizational and Judgmental Models of Cognitive Conflict Resolution," *American Psychologist,* Vol. 16 (1961), p. 409 (abstract).

Leaders' Influence on Public Opinion

discrepancy from a disliked source he is likely to *contrast* the position, and view it as more discrepant from his own than it is in fact. Contrasting a source's position is thus a way of dissociating oneself from the opinions of an unpopular source. Hence the Socialist Labor party, whose platform is based upon a version of Marxist socialism, goes to great pains to derogate the Russian communist system as "Stalinist" and "totalitarian," and to underline all of their disagreements with the Soviet system. Similarly, persons on the far right of the American political spectrum are likely to view such "liberals" as Walter Reuther, Arthur Schlesinger, Jr., and Hubert Humphrey as holding positions closer to communism and socialism than they have held in fact. By contrasting the positions of these negatively evaluated sources, consonance is created in the form of $-+-$, or perhaps $--+$.[11] The contrast form of distortion can lead to increased tension if, for some reason, the source is later more favorably evaluated. Some political opponents of President Kennedy were placed in this position following his assassination.

With this in mind, we should counsel our mayors and newspapers and leaders:

> People who differ from you will tend to distort your views. When you differ slightly from your friends, they will think you agree with them. Your enemies will think you disagree with them more than you actually do. Both tendencies will weaken your capacity to influence them in the way you wish to.

And, as time goes by, the greater will be the distortion in these directions.

We would expect, of course, that distortion would be greatest on issues of extremely high involvement. In our day, such an issue is communism. The "contrast" effect operates very strongly at both ends of the spectrum: the "anti-Communists" perceive such disparate types as socialists, communists, liberals, atheists, civil libertarians, and Supreme Court Justices as all being communists or fellow travelers; and the "anti-anti-Communists" perceive members of the John Birch Society, right-wing Republicans and Democrats, Nazis, and numerous other groups as being a good deal more similar than they really are. It is interesting that the political influence of the John Birch Society has been limited by the suspicions it has cast upon the patriotism, or intelligence, or both, of former President Eisenhower. Because of this, many conservative Republicans have derogated the Society, and especially its leader Robert Welch, as sources. They were willing to "contrast" liberal Democrats and even Earl Warren, but they wanted to "assimilate" the popular General Eisenhower as one of their own.

Incredulity. A fourth mode of dissonance reduction, rather like distortion, is "incredulity," or disbelief of the report that a given communicator has taken the dissonant position. For example, Harvey, Kelley, and Shapiro set up a situation in which acquaintances rated each other on a variety of important personality traits (such as "sociability," and "intelli-

---

[11] M. Manis, "Interpretation of Opinion Statements as a Function of Recipient Attitude and Source Prestige," *Journal of Abnormal and Social Psychology*, Vol. 63 (1961), pp. 82–86.

gence"), then received bogus ratings indicating they thought very little of each other. When the experimenters asked if they thought their friends had actually made the ratings they saw, the incredulity response appeared. The worse the ratings (and hence the greater the dissonance), the more likely a subject was to doubt that his friend had actually made the ratings.[12]

Incredulity often appears, given the ambiguous nature of many political pronouncements, in the interpretation placed upon a political leader's statement. Arguments can go far into the night on "what he *really* meant when he said . . . ," while the contestants each try to claim the statement agrees (or disagrees) with their own opinions. Many mass communications reach their audiences secondhand; a friend tells the voter about a speech he saw on television the night before, or something he read in the newspaper that morning.[13] Frequently the influence that might be generated by this ramification of a message is mitigated by incredulity. "I don't believe he could have said that. That's just not consistent with what he believes; you must be misquoting him." The frequent complaint that "he was quoted out of context" is another manifestation of the incredulity response to dissonance arousal. Some candidates, in fact, count on incredulity to maintain support among persons with relatively widely varying opinions. A presidential candidate may make a strong civil rights speech to a Negro group in the North, then a much milder speech to a white audience in the South. If the voters like the candidate, each group is more likely to judge his position on what they heard with their own ears than on rumors trickling in from a distant area. If they do not like the candidate, they are likely to believe any such rumor with even minimal substantiation. The opposition will pick up the inconsistency and broadcast it, but partisans of the speaker will often respond to this news with incredulity.

Cognitive reorganization. A fifth form of dissonance reduction is cognitive reorganization of the opinions within an opinion cluster. Reorganization sometimes takes the form of minimizing the importance or salience of dissonant opinions. If you disagree with your candidate on one issue you may turn to other issues and claim that his approach to them is so valuable it justifies overlooking his unpalatable opinions on the first issue. Or, as was the case with many supporters of the late Senator McCarthy, you may say that the end (discovering communists) was so important that he should be encouraged, despite the unhappy consequences of his means (his somewhat indiscriminate accusations of disloyalty). Perhaps in more cases than is commonly realized, support among various elements of the population is maintained by a political leader simply by encouraging this kind of cognitive juggling. Other forms of reorganization are: *making distinctions* ("he may be a dictator, but at least the trains run on time"; or, "testing 'dirty bombs' is bad but there's nothing wrong with testing 'clean

---

[12] O. J. Harvey, H. H. Kelley, and M. M. Shapiro, "Reactions to Unfavorable Evaluations of the Self Made by Other Persons," *Journal of Personality,* Vol. 25 (1957), pp. 393–411.

[13] On the importance of these personal mediators in the mass communication process, see Elihu Katz and Paul F. Lazarsfeld, *Personal Influence* (New York: The Free Press of Glencoe, 1955).

Leaders' Influence on Public Opinion

bombs'") and *bolstering* consonant opinions which are under attack ("maybe smoking does cause lung cancer, but it is extremely enjoyable, good for my nerves, socially necessary, etc.").[14]

In this section, we have suggested that each influence situation has three basic components: the respondent's opinion, his evaluation of the source of influence, and his perception of the source's position. The outcome, or mode of dissonance reduction, depends upon the resistance to change of the various cognitive elements relevant to the influence situation. The least resistant cognitive element is most likely to change. Five basic forms of dissonance reduction were described: opinion change, source re-evaluation, distortion of the source's position, incredulity, and cognitive reorganization.

As we have developed these general ideas it has become increasingly clear that political influence depends as much upon the strength of the attitudes and opinions of the audience as it does upon the skill and resources of the political leader or the newspaper or other source. Now let us examine in more detail the sources of resistance to change of the opinions held by the public.

Sources of Resistance to Opinion Change

Why doesn't a person under the strains of dissonance simply change his opinion on the subject and be done with it? The reason is that there are costs or resistances of various kinds in such opinion changes. A person may resist changing his opinion for any one of the following reasons:

1. The opinion is one he has tested by experience; he "knows" it to be true. If he were to give up this perception of reality, he would have to doubt his senses, or repudiate his past, or change his epistemology.

2. There is an authority or a source for his opinion which is even more highly valued than the source that seeks to persuade him to change. Opinions and values learned in one's childhood are often highly resistant to change for this reason.

3. The opinion is anchored in group membership which he values, or is the opinion of a reference group with which he identifies. Giving up the opinion threatens some part of what these groups mean to him; or at least he may interpret his situation that way. As they found out in the army, the de-grouped person in the replacement depot was more amenable to opinion change than the person in a unit which constantly "cued him in."

4. The individual has a public stake in his opinion. A number of studies have shown that a person is more malleable if he has only committed himself privately than if he has stated his position publicly. In the latter case, *his* reputation is at stake. And if someone advocates the same position for years, it becomes very difficult to reverse.

[14] R. P. Abelson, "Modes of Resolution of Belief Dilemmas," *Journal of Conflict Resolution,* Vol. 3 (1959), pp. 343–352.

5. The opinion serves some social function for the individual: it helps him to make friends, eases social friction, makes him appear better in other people's eyes.

6. The opinion serves some economic function for the individual; by opposing heavy taxation the businessman promotes for himself and his friends a situation permitting him to retain a larger share of his income.

7. The opinion serves an intra-psychic function; it offers a "legitimate" target for his aggression; permits him to win a chronic internalized war against his dead father, provides a respectable façade for things he is ashamed of and has long repressed.[15]

8. The opinion rationalizes some role-strain in which he finds himself; it accounts for his difficulties and gives him an ethical base and denigrates his critics so that he can carry out his social role with a supporting belief system.[16]

It is for these reasons, that the mass persuasive powers of a political leader or of a newspaper are usually small. These eight are the mediating factors to which Klapper refers when he says: "Mass communication *ordinarily* does not serve as a necessary and sufficient cause of audience effects, but rather functions among and through a nexus of mediating factors and influences."[17] These "factors and influences" modify and reduce the possibilities for the management of opinion in a free society. But, perhaps there is still room for such management.

Reputation in the Political Process

The foregoing discussion of persuasion should have made it plain that the two most important variables in an influence situation are the resistance to change of the respondent's opinion and his evaluation of the source. In a broader sense, the latter depends very much upon the source's reputation. Now let us turn to the question of what a reputation consists of.

Banfield, in speaking of the "civic leader,"—a role he finds especially significant in the influence processes of the seven case studies he examines —says, "In the main, the influence of these 'civic leaders' derives from the trust that others have in their judgment and in their disinterestedness."[18] Civic leaders have other functions as well; they can negotiate behind the scenes, they can advise the political head, but even here their strength lies in part in their reputation, something they must conserve if they are to have influence on future occasions. This, then, is one kind of reputation.

Another kind is suggested by the fact that, according to Banfield, the Mayor of Chicago is usually the chairman of the county Democratic com-

[15] For analysis of social, economic, and intra-psychic functions, see M. Brewster Smith, Jerome S. Bruner, and Robert W. White, *Opinions and Personality* (New York: Wiley, 1956).

[16] See Francis X. Sutton and associates, *The American Business Creed* (Cambridge: Harvard University Press, 1956).

[17] Joseph T. Klapper, *The Effects of Mass Communication* (New York: The Free Press of Glencoe, 1960), p. 8.

[18] Edward C. Banfield, *Political Influence* (New York: The Free Press of Glencoe, 1961), p. 282.

Leaders' Influence on Public Opinion

mittee and "therefore the leading figure in the party in Illinois and one of its leading figures nationally." In order to fill these roles adequately (and to get the needed votes from the areas outside Chicago), the Mayor and his party must create a reputation as a "force for clean and progressive government."[19] Here is another politically important kind of reputation.

Dahl quotes a political leader as saying:

> You have to be liked. . . . I do a lot of things for people. I keep working at it. . . . People come to see me, call me at my home at night. For instance a woman calls me, her husband has gone out and got drunk, and he's arrested for drunken driving. She can't meet bail. She calls me up and I go down and bail him out. . . . I'm always building up loyalty.[20]

There then is a reputation among a special clientele and its friends and acquaintances.

Newspapers, as well as individuals, have reputations. Of the New Haven newspapers, Dahl says:

> With all their advantages of easy entry into New Haven households, the Jackson (New Haven) papers suffer from the distinct handicap of being widely regarded as politically biased and even eccentric. . . . In our interviews, leaders regularly denied that the local papers had any influence on their views or those of their friends. . . . Thus the Jackson papers tend to lack one of the important prerequisites of successful persuasion, confidence in the source.[21]

Referring to our previous chapter, on group influence, we may recall that one of the conditions of group influence was the appraisal of the group by its members—that is, its reputation. What we have to say about the reputation of an influence source could apply to a man, a group, or the media.

Reputation itself, however, is an ambiguous concept. Consider four possibilities, based on personal, group, ethical, and technical considerations:

1. Personal loyalty, as with the political leader mentioned above. The reverse of this, of course, would be a personal opposition, perhaps because of some disfavor received.

2. Partisan loyalty, as when a person represents a class of people or group to whom the respondent is attached—party, ethnic group, region, race, etc. (Mayor Daley's inner-core support in Chicago has this quality.)

3. Ethical trust, as with a judge, where the basis of the support is the belief that the source will develop or administer a formula which uses the common ethical norms of a society. (Banfield's "civil leader" is endowed with some of this confidence.)

4. Technical trust, as with a physician, where the basis is confidence in the superior technical information of the source. (For his outside-Chicago following, Mayor Daley must develop such an image.)

---

[19] *Ibid.*, pp. 245, 246.
[20] Robert A. Dahl, *Who Governs?* (New Haven: Yale University Press, 1961), p. 249.
[21] *Ibid.*, pp. 258–259.

In an over-all sense, however, all four of these have one thing in common: they are either positive or negative. Therefore, a message from one of these leaders (or from a newspaper, or some group norm) comes to an audience bearing some advantage or disadvantage. It is either more persuasive, or less so, because of its source. Let us examine this further.

Political Influence and Persuasion

Political influence is the command over resources which can be used to change behavior of people who are important in some decision-making process. One of these resources is "reputation," the public image of a man, or, since he has many publics, the plural "images" he projects. When he is the vehicle of communication, the source of a message, he may well produce dissonance in some part of his publics. Attentive to the social sciences, perhaps he seeks to make use of their findings for political ends. What does he do?

He does what all politicians do, he attempts to build up loyalties, trust, some love and some fear (as Machiavelli would say). He uses this reputation wisely, conserving his unpopular statements for crucial moments.

He manipulates distortion, relying on the assimilation effect and minimizing the contrast effect among his publics.

He manipulates incredulity, using it as a cover for his varied and conflicting appeals to opposing groups.

He encourages such cognitive reorganization as will suit his ends: shifting from a focus on ends to a focus on means, changing the salience of issues, creating new distinctions to show where he is different from his opponent, originating new concepts that place his proposals in a different and more favorable light.

He attacks the resistances to his opinions indirectly. He seeks out those whose ties with hostile groups have been already weakened and directs his appeal to them. He denigrates (or has his henchman do it) the opposing authorities. He shows why previous commitments are no longer relevant. He makes his catchwords, his slogans, the vehicle of social communication and "phatic communion." He provides formulas for easing specific reference group conflicts and specific well diagnosed role-strains. He suggests other targets for the hostile, reassures the insecure, invites the lonely into his party, tells everyone that he loves them.

In short, he creates consonance where there was dissonance. Can the "scientific" politician do better than his "natural" opponent? In the next decade, we shall see.

Opinion
Without
Information

Level of Information and Opinion

Democracy places a burden of thought upon the public
more onerous than the burden placed upon it by other systems.
What must a public know in order for its members to be
able to carry out their civic roles with adequacy?
Or perhaps, we should ask: Who must be able to use what knowledge
in what way? Our following examination of the many facets of opinion
and information initiates an understanding of these questions.

On a variety of cultural matters, in spite of their greater number of years in school, Americans are less informed than the British. Asked in 1955 to identify ten such names as Columbus, Shakespeare, Napoleon, Beethoven, Karl Marx, Rubens, the British public showed a higher level of information on all except Columbus. (AIPO, 11/27–28/55) On another educational front, the nature of public literacy, we find the Canadian public better than the Americans; in a kind of international spelling bee conducted by the Gallup organizations, the Canadians did better than the Americans. (AIPO, 9/24/55, 12/24/55) Perhaps some of the difference is due to the fact that American adults tend to stop reading books after they leave school; at least according to postwar surveys relatively fewer adults in America read books than do adults in England, Sweden, or Denmark.[1] Taken altogether, these kinds of comparisons raise questions about the quality of the American educational system.

On the other hand, although we do not have comparable data on political information, there is some evidence to show that Americans at least seek it as much as do the British and other Europeans. They read a daily newspaper in about the same proportions[2] and a recent study reports that they seek out political information in the news much more than do the French. When comparable national samples in America and France were asked about their frequency of newspaper reading for political information, 44 per cent of the Americans replied "regularly," while only about 19 per cent of the French said "regulierement." Appraising these and other data, Converse and Dupeux report, "there seems little doubt of the higher American devotion to newspapers as a source of political information. Furthermore, the French citizen appears also to monitor other media for political information less."[3] Much of this, it seems, is due to the smaller number of people in America without high school education. Thus there is some evidence that although with regard to certain kinds of cultural information the American public is relatively uninformed, the level of political information here is as high as it is in other parts of the world. What is this information level?

There are many kinds of information, of course; let us consider some evidence of public knowledge of: (a) political leaders, (b) political issues, (c) "what the government is doing" in several fields, and (d) political institutions. On the question of knowledge of political leaders, it was found that in June, 1952, two months before he was nominated for President, Adlai Stevenson was unknown to 66 per cent of the public. In August of that year, just after the conventions, with their attendant publicity, 55 per cent of the public did not know the name of the Republican vice-presidential candidate, Richard Nixon, and 68 per cent did not know the name of the Democratic vice-presidential candidate, John Sparkman. In contrast to this, the fact that in 1955, 43 per cent of the public could iden-

[1] Hadley Cantril and Mildred Strunk, *Public Opinion 1935–46* (Princeton: Princeton University Press, 1951), pp. 48–53.

[2] *Ibid.,* p. 515.

[3] Philip E. Converse and Georges Dupeux, "Politicization of the Electorate in France and the United States," *Public Opinion Quarterly,* Vol. 26 (1962), p. 6.

Opinion Without Information

tify Marshall Tito, the President of Yugoslavia, seems rather impressive.[4] He is much better known, for example, than a man in an older generation to whom he owes something of a debt—Karl Marx. Only about 33 per cent of the American adult population could identify that name in the Cold War year, 1955 (AIPO, 11/27/55).

Awareness of issues in the news fluctuates within broad limits. One of the most hotly disputed laws in recent years was the Taft-Hartley Act, passed over President Truman's veto in 1947 and a chronic political issue in 1948, 1950, and to some extent, in 1952. The act imposed certain restrictions on labor unions, who termed the measure a "slave labor" law and campaigned for its repeal for many years. Yet in 1952, 30 per cent of the public had not heard of it (SRC, 1952). On the other hand, in 1948, 52 per cent of the public could describe the Marshall Plan; a few years later about 54 per cent could roughly describe the meaning of the farm price support program, and in several surveys, a little over half the population could consistently describe Cold War with reasonable accuracy (AIPO 1948, 1950, 1951). The reverse of this, of course, is something to think about: during the Korean War, about half the population had not grasped the meaning of the over-all term used to describe our conflict with our major opponent.

What is the government doing with respect to foreign aid, housing, integration? As might be expected, many people are quite uninformed; but this does not prevent some from saying what the government should do. This relationship between information and opinion is well reflected in a set of data gathered by the Survey Research Center in their 1956 election study:

Issue	No Opinion	Hold Opinion But Do Not Know What Gov't Is Doing	Hold Opinion and Know What Gov't Is Doing
FOREIGN POLICY			
The United States should be willing to go more than halfway in being friendly with the other countries of the world.	12%	10%	78%
This country would be better off if we just stayed home and did not concern ourselves with problems in other parts of the world.	14	15	71
The United States should keep soldiers overseas where they can help countries that are against communism.	20	13	67

[4] Hazel Gaudet Erskine has collected these survey findings and other related material in "The Polls: The Informed Public," *Public Opinion Quarterly*, Vol. 26 (1962), pp. 668–677.

Opinion Without Information

Issue	No Opinion	Hold Opinion But Do Not Know What Gov't Is Doing	Hold Opinion and Know What Gov't Is Doing
FOREIGN POLICY (cont.)			
The United States should give help to foreign countries even if they are not as much against communism as we are.	28	19	53
DOMESTIC POLICY			
If cities and towns around the country need help to build more schools, the government in Washington ought to give them the money they need.	10	23	67
If Negroes *are not* getting fair treatment in jobs and housing, the government in Washington should see to it that they do.	14	19	67
The government ought to leave things like electric power and housing for private businessmen to handle.	30	19	51
The government ought to fire any government worker who is accused of being a communist even though they can't prove it.	16	39	45

Source: Angus Campbell, Philip E. Converse, Warren E. Miller, and Donald E. Stokes, *The American Voter* (New York: Wiley, 1960), p. 174.

On all of these issues, more than half of the public had an opinion based upon some minimum knowledge of governmental policy and action. Yet from 10 to 39 per cent were willing to offer opinions unsupported by much information on what was actually going on. Shortly we shall examine some of the reasons for this drive toward opinionation; in the meantime we must observe that one of the most important kinds of knowledge is the knowledge of the appropriate informational grounds for opinions, the knowledge of one's own ignorance. Perhaps this is "modesty"; if so, what level of modesty do we want in the electoral public? One might ponder the implications, particularly for "the democratic class struggle," of the following modest comment by a woman who was asked if she ever discussed politics: "No," she said, "since I don't understand too much about politics, I just keep my mouth closed. . . . People should know what they are talking about and this takes an education which goes beyond the high school level."[5]

[5] Morris Rosenberg, "Some Determinants of Political Apathy," *Public Opinion Quarterly*, Vol. 18 (1954–55), pp. 353–354.

Opinion Without Information

There is a kind of "civics" knowledge of political institutions which has been assumed to be the foundation of an attachment to the American political system—but, of course that is wrong. Attachment to the system comes in other ways; it comes from early loyalties to the society (not the polity) of which one is a member: from moralized references of parents, from fear of deviance and ostracism, from leading a more or less gratifying life, from the rewards of compliance, obedience, conformity. These— rather than an individually worked out critique of politics—underlie citizenly loyalty and duty. It is just as well, because there are very considerable gaps in public knowledge of the way the government works:

Question	Correct Answers
What do you know about the Bill of Rights? Do you know anything it says? (NORC, Nov. 1945)	21%
How many senators are there in Washington from your state? (AIPO 8/8/45)	55%
What is meant by the electoral college? (AIPO 2/2/55)	35%
Will you tell me what the three branches of the Federal Government are called? (AIPO 3/3/54)	19%
Will you tell me what the term "veto" means to you? For example, what does it mean when the President vetoes a bill sent him by Congress. (AIPO 6/8/47)	80%

In general it is true that the younger groups, which are also the better educated, know more than the older groups, perhaps because they are closest to their school days, when these things may have been talked about. In Lane's interviews with working- and lower middle-class men it appeared that such questions as these indeed smacked of "school knowledge" as contrasted to "life knowledge" and as such carried with them the faint coloration of dry, useless information. Few life decisions hinge upon them and their implications for policy matters men care about, though really enormous, are thoroughly obscure to most of the public.

A review of this information picture tends to dishearten some students of government and partisans of the democratic system. A little over a third of the people know the names of their own congressman (AIPO 8/13/47), and a little less than half know which party controls Congress and thus which party is "responsible" for the legislative record.[6] A large proportion do not know the centrally important issues at any one time; most people are unaware of the nature and meaning of the Bill of Rights, the central features of the electoral system, the names of the three branches of government. Moreover: (1) From other studies it is clear that more people are willing to report on what the government ought to be doing than are able to say what it is doing, revealing an important informational gap. (2) The relatively low amount of information possessed by most persons means that most must decide their political preferences on the basis of comparatively simple slogans and catchwords, since the more subtle

[6] Donald E. Stokes and Warren E. Miller, "Party Government and the Saliency of Congress," *Public Opinion Quarterly*, Vol. 26 (1962), pp. 531–546.

analysis will pass them by. And, finally (3) this level of information reinforces our emphasis upon the importance of external social referents in opinion formation and change. If a person is unable to decide for himself, he must go on the basis of some reference in the social world, such as a union leader, an ethnic spokesman, the opinion "down at the shop" or "in the office," and particularly the position of a political party. Beyond these familiar referents there are the statements of great and trusted public personalities.

Who Knows? Individual and Group Differences

In general, as we have noted, younger people are better informed on most civic matters, but, as a matter of fact, this advantage does not extend to the names of political figures, particularly representatives and senators. Rural groups tend to be less well-informed on most issues, but again, they tend to be better-informed on the names of their representatives; indeed, they seem to personalize politics in a way reminiscent of more traditional and less economically developed societies. Men, of course, are better-informed than women (though this difference tends to disappear in rural areas); after all, politics is thought to be more of a man's sphere of competence. And, of course, the better educated are better-informed than the less well-educated and the difference between college and high school is greater than the difference between high school and grade school. Education is the most important of all factors in sorting out the informed from the ignorant.[7]

There is something about this educational factor, however, which needs to be cleared up. It is possible that having had a college education increases one's zeal to "keep up" with current affairs, but it is equally possible that persons who have gone to college come from families which were more concerned with current affairs, were able to afford, and were interested in, more literature on current events (news magazines, for example), and hence that these differences were produced by factors other than education itself.

The second of these conclusions is suggested, though not unequivocally proven, by a recent study by McClintock and Turner. They compared the political information of freshmen and seniors at seven California colleges and universities. They found that if sex and grade point average were held constant, no significant differences at all obtained between freshmen and seniors. The freshmen were every bit as well-informed as the seniors. Seniors with low grade point averages were somewhat better-informed than freshmen with low grade point averages—but then such seniors were former freshmen who at least had not flunked out of school.[8]

The McClintock-Turner study perhaps is not the best test of the effects of a college education on political information, for a variety of

[7] See Erskine, op. cit.

[8] C. G. McClintock. and H. A. Turner, "The Impact of College upon Political Knowledge, Participation, and Values," *Human Relations*, Vol. 15 (1962), pp. 163–176.

Opinion Without Information

reasons. The mass media may be more accessible to the high school student living at home than to the college student living in a dormitory. The college student also has more of his intellectual energy wrapped up in passing his courses than does the college graduate. A variety of such reasons may make this not a perfect test. Yet the study certainly shows that a college education does not produce an enormous informational increment in the student's political thinking. The notion that it has a delayed-action effect, in inspiring greater curiosity and motivation to learn, awaits further testing.

Of course it would be interesting, and would serve certain partisan ends, if it could be demonstrated that people who held one ideological position were regularly better-informed than their opponents. Would it be the case, for example, that conservatives tended to be better-informed than liberals? Some time ago, particularly during the 'thirties, it was thought that the opposite was true, that liberals tended consistently in colleges and high schools to be better informed than conservatives. A more careful study by G. H. Smith, however, sorted out the various components of liberalism and found that the relationship between information and both support of civil-rights legislation and a moderate attitude toward the Soviet Union was very close. On the other hand, the relationship between being informed and support of (a) unions and of (b) government guarantees of economic support to all citizens was either negligible or negative. This was one of many studies showing that there are two kinds of liberalism: the civil libertarian and internationalist variety, and welfare-state liberalism. At least in the student population the first kind of liberals are better-informed than their opponents, but the second kind have no such advantage.[9]

Seeking and Avoiding Information

While it is true, as we have remarked, that it is one thing to be informed and something else to have an opinion, certain circumstances tend to bring these together and to require informed opinions. One of these circumstances is the responsibility for action based upon opinion. This is the position of the civil servant and the executive and, sometimes, the legislator. It is the position of the aristocrat in an elitist society, but "for most people in modern society, there is no such direct relation between responsibility for having an opinion and responsibility for action."[10] In one sense, then, we must say that modern society has divorced the pressure to have an opinion from the pressure to be informed; it has kept the one and eroded the other.

[9] C. Robert Pace, "The Relationship Between Liberalism and Knowledge of Current Affairs," *Journal of Social Psychology*, Vol. 10 (1939), pp. 247–258; Willard A. Kerr, "Correlates of Politico-Economic Liberalism-Conservatism," *Journal of Social Psychology*, Vol. 20 (1944), pp. 61–77; G. H. Smith and Joel Dobin, "Information and Politico-Economic Opinions," *Public Opinion Quarterly*, Vol. 12 (1948), pp. 731–733.

[10] David Riesman and Nathan Glazer, "The Meaning of Opinion," *Public Opinion Quarterly*, Vol. 12 (1948–49), p. 635.

Yet this is not an accurate picture either, for there are ways in which society presses toward *informed* opinions not dependent upon responsibility for government action. One of these is the judgment of peers against what may be called "the blowhard" or "the loudmouth," that is, the opinionated and ignorant. Another is the very process of opinion formation in which stating an opinion provides a vested interest which then invites inquiry into sources of support for that vested opinion-interest. A third is the internalized standards for proper opinionation—standards on which our schools are sometimes tragically vague.

But in the immediate discussion we will focus less on social pressures than on individual desires and will consider the drives for information as partly counterbalanced by the drives pressing toward withdrawal and a posture of "don't know," perhaps with a "don't care" thrown in. In each case we might ask, paraphrasing Smith, Bruner, and White, "Of what use to a man is his information?"[11] Looking at the positive side of the balance, first, one finds a most general answer in the idea of a drive to structure and understand the world in which a man lives. It is said that "the individual tries to reconcile conflicting impressions, seeks to know what the world is like, and to make sense out of it."[12] Without further compensation, this is reward in itself, or at least the implied psychic ease which it brings is rewarding. Adding to this idea, Smith suggests that the function of the effort to know the world is more particularly to help a person to "order his life."[13] But there are more directly instrumental uses of information gathering. A good way to see this in human detail is to see what people miss when they cannot get it. One instance was when, in a newspaper strike before the widespread use of television, they were deprived of a regular source. Berelson reports it in these terms, quoting from his respondents to make the deprivation more vivid.[14]

What do people use a newspaper for?

For information about and interpretation of public affairs: I miss the detail and the explanation of events leading up to the news. I like to get the story behind and the development leading up to (it)—it's more penetrating.

As a tool for daily living: [Here comments referred to the newspaper as a guide to radio programs, movie offerings, financial reports, obituaries, weather forecasts, etc.]

For respite: I didn't know what to do with myself. I was depressed. There was nothing to read and pass the time. I got a paper on Wednesday and felt a whole lot better.

[11] See M. Brewster Smith, Jerome S. Bruner, and Robert W. White, *Opinions and Personality* (New York: Wiley, 1956), p. 1.

[12] See Irving Sarnoff, Daniel Katz, and Charles McClintock, "Attitude-Change Procedures and Motivating Patterns," in Daniel Katz and others, (eds.), *Public Opinion and Propaganda* (New York: Dryden, 1954), p. 305.

[13] M. Brewster Smith, "The Personal Setting of Public Opinions: A Study of Attitudes Toward Russia," *Public Opinion Quarterly*, Vol. 11 (1947–48), pp. 507–523.

[14] Bernard Berelson, "What 'Missing the Newspaper' Means," in Katz and others (eds.), *op. cit.*, pp. 263–271.

Opinion Without Information

For social prestige and communication: You have to read in order to keep up a conversation with other people. It is embarrassing not to know if you are in company who discuss the news.

For [vicarious] social contact: I missed them (favorite columnists) for their information, their news, their interviews with various people. It is interesting to know people's reactions. If you read the background of individuals, you can analyze them a little better.

To relieve general anxiety: I am like a fish out of water. . . . I am lost and nervous. I'm ashamed to admit it. I feel awfully lost. I like the feeling of being in touch with the world at large.

The selection of information serves other motives. Information may be sought as an aggressive weapon against others; it is useful for the person, and a prominent feature of the academic population, whose main source of self-esteem is in "being right"; there are collectors of information who use it in a fetishistic way, each item is libidinized and lovingly stored away in the memory; and there are those who use information selectively to reinforce an ideological framework which is inaccessible to uncongenial knowledge.

But, as we said, a person's collection of information is the product, not of a thirst for knowledge, however distorted, but of a balance between the need to know and other needs, including the need not to find out. The most obvious of these "ignoration" needs, is the need to conserve time and energy for other purposes, a situation where knowledge does not have a negative value, but rather a lower priority. In Lane's interviews with working-class men, some explained their lack of civic information in terms of their other responsibilities.

A special case of the preoccupation with other matters is the person with low self-esteem. Such a man has trouble interacting with others; he is fearful of the impression he is making and he becomes self-conscious in their presence. But he might well make up for this with greater newspaper reading and information gathering, and while some do this, the evidence shows that most don't. "Why," asks Morris Rosenberg about the person with low self-esteem, "is he less *interested* in public affairs?" He answers his question with some data on the basis of interviews with high school juniors and seniors in New York State. "People with low self-esteem," he says, "are more likely than others to retreat into a private world of daydreaming. Whereas 59 per cent of them were high on a Guttman scale of daydreaming, this was only true of 13 per cent of those with high self-esteem."[15] In a more general way, too, they report that "I often find that I am distracted from public affairs by my personal problems." In short, they are too busy, with a special kind of self-involved busyness.

A third kind of general informational avoidance, at least within a wide range, has to do with the stimulus properties of information. In Berelson's interviews there were some, though not very many, who found relief in the lack of newspapers. As one person put it, "It was rather a relief not to have my nerves upset by stories of murders, rape, divorce, and

[15] Morris Rosenberg, "Self-Esteem and Concern with Public Affairs," *Public Opinion Quarterly*, Vol. 26 (1962), pp. 210–211.

Opinion Without Information

the war." And another person commented "I've been reading [Korean] war news so much, I've had enough of it."[16] For the anxious and insecure, or perhaps merely the very sensitive, news can grate upon the nerves.

But there are people who reject certain kinds of information because it is positively threatening to them. In *Political Life*, Lane suggests several varieties of this rejection. There is *cathartic ignorance*, where a person needs his unchallenged biases in order to give vent to a charge of angry feelings about, say, "the bureaucrats" or "those red-baiters." There is *status quo ignorance*, based upon a satisfaction with things as they are, and hence a rejection of information which might challenge the situation. The burden of proof (evidence and argument) is thus thrust upon the reformer. There is a *socializing ignorance*, the counterpart of the need for information for social communication which Berelson illustrates in his study. Ignorance of the unpopular fact prevents a man from making a social gaffe. These three varieties are, in fact, variations of the need for avoiding the dissonance discussed earlier; but there is a fourth kind: *privatizing ignorance*. One of the tensions of citizenship is the conflict between public and private life. The rejection of intrusive public demands upon private life could well lead a man to say "Enough! I don't want to know any more."[17]

All of these fall into a pattern of selective inattention to or rejection of certain kinds of information, but occasionally there is a special mechanism at work: intolerance of ambiguity. Else Frenkel-Brunswik has found that one of the characteristics of the authoritarian personality is this intolerance of ambiguity—ambiguous drawings, unresolved situations, indecisive men.[18] Certainly men marked by this characteristic will ignore the information favoring a choice they have rejected, information which would impose upon them that thing to be most dreaded—doubt.

Information Must Be Thought About

The same "bit" of information is highly useful in some minds—useless in others. The difference, of course, lies in how it is connected to other information, opinions, values. The connecting process is nothing other than *thinking*, something we must touch on briefly here.

One of the things that will make a bit of information useful is *familiarity with an appropriate concept* or category to put it in; without that it may not be noticed, for it may not have much meaning. A man sees in the papers that a local utility has raised its prices and the significance is limited to his regret over his larger outlay. If he is aware of the concept "monopoly" (and 64 per cent of the public has a rough understanding of the meaning of this term—AIPO 6/10/50) there is the possibility of an enlarged understanding. Another man sees the federal gov-

16 Berelson, *op. cit.*, p. 270.

17 Robert E. Lane, *Political Life: Why People Get Involved in Politics* (New York: The Free Press of Glencoe, 1959), pp. 113–114.

18 Else Frenkel-Brunswik, "Intolerance of Ambiguity, as an Emotional and Personality Variable," *Journal of Personality*, Vol. 18 (1949), pp. 108–143.

Opinion Without Information

ernment undertake a new service for dependent mothers. If he is among the 36 per cent of the public that can define the term "welfare state," he can more easily put this new bit of information into a framework with broader meaning, and generalize its significance. Thus, the understanding of a wide variety of concepts is, perhaps, the first step in putting information to use.

The comprehension of such concepts, of course, is a product of education and interest. On this latter score, the focus of interest of the public is reflected by the fact that in a 1950 test the three best understood concepts and the three least understood concepts, with the percentages of the public able to define them, were as follows:

Flying saucers	94%
Universal military training	75
Bookie	68
Reciprocal trade agreements	29
Bipartisan foreign policy	26
Point Four	5

(AIPO 6/10/50)

But conceptual clarity implies more than familiarity with a term, or approximating a dictionary definition; it may also imply *concept formation*. What shall we do, for example with the concept "good citizen," mixing, as it does, an evaluative component with an understanding of a social role? Lane asked his sample of working-class men to say what they thought the term meant. Everybody "knew," but everybody had a different definition, some seeing it as meaning a good, honest, sincere man, others as a friendly person who helped in common neighborhood tasks, others as a good family man, others as a person who fulfilled his political duties faithfully, and still others as a person who did not criticize society. These men were faced with two problems, each illustrating an aspect of conceptualization in political discourse. First, they were confronted with the fact that there is no consensus on the citizen's role in Eastport, where they lived, just as there may be no consensus on the meaning of, say, "imperialism" in international society. It is not necessarily the case that for every word there is an agreed upon referent, something "out there" for which the word is an appropriate symbol. Under these circumstances, everyone creates his own and a babble of voices may result. Political argument and thought as often founder on this obstacle as on the obstacle created by poverty of information.

And second, even if everyone knew exactly what "citizen" meant, there were differences in evaluation, due to the different values each brought to the problem. Value clarity is as important as empirical clarity (defining real world phenomena) in political thinking. It is just as important to ask "What do you mean by 'good'?" as it is to ask "What do you mean by 'citizen'?" Concept formation and concept clarity have at least these two aspects, the empirical and the evaluational.

Third, there is the problem of *concept attainment*, that is, assigning instances to a category or concept.[19] Is Thomas Jefferson a good citizen? Is Aaron Burr? Is John Doe? Are you? A good definition makes it easier, but it often is very difficult, particularly when an object can "earn" concept attainment in several alternative (disjunctive) ways. One strategy is to take the several criteria of the definition and demand evidence enough on each of them to allow some assignment. But what is enough evidence? How much evidence on a person's loyalty is needed to assign him as a "good citizen" to a sensitive job in the Department of Defense? Another way is to look for patterns or consistencies in the various criteria. For example, a person is likely to be a regular voter if he volunteers to canvass in an election, because voting almost always goes along with canvassing (but not vice versa). A third test, not a very good one but often all there is, is the test by consensus. "Such categories as 'good citizens' or 'decent fellow' are often in effect consensually validated."[20] And finally, particularly in such emotional areas as patriotism and citizenship, there is a purely subjective test, an inner feeling of certainty. Such "tests" are incapable of disproof, of course, and are expressive in their nature. The degree to which any given public relies upon this fourth kind of test is a measure of its unreadiness for the burden of effective citizenship.

If a person has some information and some more or less clear concepts into which it fits, he is ready to do a little political thinking. His success along these lines depends a good deal on his ideas of causation, especially social causation. Answers to the question "Why?" are causal answers. Policies are advocated because people think certain laws or governmental acts will cause or bring about preferred events—say, prosperity. In this connection, perhaps the most important differences are to be found among those who rely upon (1) fate or chance, or (2) personal agents, "good" or "bad" leaders, or (3) impersonal circumstances or social forces. In asking his sample of working-class men, "what causes war" and "what causes poverty" and "what causes delinquency?" Lane found that relatively few Americans shrug their shoulders and blame "fate" or refer to "Divine providence"; that is the way of the traditional societies of the less developed areas and these societies' passive subjects. On the other hand, many tended to explain everything in terms of the personal qualities of political leaders, their greed, or their stupidity, or their sincerity. Such men also tended to blame poverty upon the poor. Personalized explanations of this kind were not too helpful, for they led up blind alleys when it came to discussions of reform and, moreover, opened up the possibility that change could only be achieved through some "Great Leader." On the other hand, those who saw wars as the products of, say, population pressures, or believed poverty to be caused by the working of an uncontrolled business cycle, opened up avenues of reform through the usual processes of a representative government adjusting a delicate economic mechanism or offering medical assistance to those in need. Those relying on these impersonal concepts

[19] The following discussion relies upon some of the formulations in Jerome S. Bruner, Jacqueline J. Goodnow, and George A. Austin, *A Study of Thinking* (New York: Wiley, 1956), particularly pp. 17–22.

68   [20] *Ibid.*, p. 19.

of cause were not only the more intelligent, but also had a better command over their own impulses.[21]

Finally, if a man has a piece of information, some useful concepts and a grasp on the nature of social causation, there is still the context into which his information is placed. He may employ some well-formulated belief system to give the information "meaning"; that is, to draw inferences about what is going on and what should be done. Everyone has some belief system references of this kind (democratic, socialist, isolationist, etc.). The big difference comes, as we have mentioned before, between those who use all information selectively to bolster a rigid belief system (dogmatists) and those more open to information which challenges their belief system.[22] A more open belief system, such as Lane found his respondents had, gave less help in interpreting events, but also it served less to block new information.

The value of information is often cumulative; within a given field of knowledge, each new "bit" gives added value to related "bits." Knowing the name of a candidate for President may be useless unless one also knows his party, because, for many people, the party label is a cue which tells them who is "for" him. Beyond that, a knowledge of what the candidate stands for may give his name and party additional meaning. In Elmira in 1948 a study found, however, that "only about one third of the voters are highly accurate in their perception of where the candidates stand on the issues," and that others misjudge at least one of four important issues on which the candidates could be assigned positions.[23] Thus they could not link issue and name. But the point can be made with "larger" decisions. Lane asked his sample of working-class men about their opinions on American policy toward the Soviet Union. The wiser respondents did three things. (1) They anticipated Russian responses to American policy, that is, they had an idea of "feedback"; (2) they placed the American policy in a historical framework, that is, they could embrace a longer time period and hence anticipate delayed reactions, and (3) they compared American policy with the policies of other nations; they used a comparative approach, finding, in this search process, alternatives to be weighed and considered.[24] As students of public opinion, therefore, we need to know not merely the extent of the public's information, but the structure of this information, the interrelationships among the informational "bits" which create a pattern of meaning and interpretation.

We have found the informational level of the American public to be rather low; somewhat less adequate to its tasks than has sometimes been imagined. But, as we have tried to show, the level of information possessed by a public achieves its significance in the uses to which it is put. Here lies the major problem of education for democracy, or, as it is now called, the

[21] Robert E. Lane, *Political Ideology: Why the American Common Man Believes What He Does* (New York: The Free Press of Glencoe, 1962), pp. 308–309.

[22] See Milton Rokeach, *The Open and Closed Mind* (New York: Basic Books, 1960).

[23] Bernard Berelson, Paul F. Lazarsfeld, and William N. McPhee, *Voting* (Chicago: University of Chicago Press, 1954), p. 233.

[24] Lane, *Political Ideology*, pp. 350–356.

socialization process. Pouring "civics" into the electorate won't help much (it won't be remembered long, either); teaching men how to use knowledge, how to conceptualize, appraise evidence, infer causality—there lies a task worthy of a great teacher.

Opinions Often Come before Information and Reasons

There is something about this whole process of knowing and thinking about politics which has been treated indirectly on many occasions but now must be faced directly. Do people first decide who or what they are for, and then seek information and arguments to support that position? Or do they acquire information and after thinking about its implications, then decide who or what they are for? It is an inter-active process, of course, going back and forth between preference and reason and, perhaps, changed preference, but the importance of inherited political party identification, the use of reference groups in framing an opinion, and the importance of special intra-psychic gratifications derived from certain opinions suggest that a very frequent order is: opinions first, information and reasons later. Now we have strong experimental evidence to support this.

Rosenberg has described two studies in which he implanted, by hypnotic induction, a reversal of the emotional feelings attached to a public issue. For example, one of his subjects had been against Negroes living in white neighborhoods. In the hypnotic induction, the subject was told, "When you awake, you will be very much in favor of Negroes moving into white neighborhoods. The mere idea of Negroes moving into white neighborhoods will give you a happy, exhilarated feeling."[25]

Rosenberg presents ample evidence to show that the hypnotic inductions were effective in reversing the directions of opinions on the issue. For example, this subject then genuinely favored Negroes living in white neighborhoods. More than that, Rosenberg showed that this change was a product of two separate changes in the subjects' thinking. First, they changed their *values* to correspond with their changed attitudes toward Negroes and whites living in the same neighborhood. Second, they changed their ideas of how these values could best be *implemented*, that is, put into practice. As a result, the organization of their thoughts and attitudes was changed by the hypnotic suggestion and a new system of ideas was created to support their changed outlook. In doing this they "discovered" many new arguments for integration which they had not thought about before.

Rosenberg's implantation of radical affective changes toward particular attitude objects was stronger and more rapid than is customary in political life. However, it has very clear implications for those cases in which people learn strong "feelings" (of favor or disfavor) about some attitude object without knowing much about it, or without having much in the way of supporting knowledge. From Rosenberg's research, we can expect

25 Milton J. Rosenberg, "An Analysis of Affective-Cognitive Consistency," in Carl I. Hovland and M. J. Rosenberg (eds.), *Attitude Organization and Change* (New Haven: Yale University Press, 1960).

Opinion Without Information

that such people will, over time, collect and develop cognitions which will bolster their preferences and will be consistent with them. In a sense, they will "rationalize" the unfavorable or favorable feeling they have by adducing reasons why it is a desirable position.

For example, many Southern white children grow up thinking that Negroes are morally and intellectually inferior, as a race, to Caucasians. These opinions have their origins, of course, both in parental opinions and in the dominant beliefs of the childhood social environment. They are reasonably strongly developed before the child reaches high school; i.e., before he is in an intellectual position to evaluate the matter on a scientific basis. As the child grows up, many challenges to this belief, and to the social system it creates, are issued, many, in particular, by the federal government or by the federal judiciary. The cognitive elaboration of these simple affective tendencies has, however, produced in the subsequent years a comprehensive political ideology concerning the constitutional basis of state vs. federal powers, and so forth. In time, therefore, the individual may well come to think that his position on segregation is based upon a rational consideration of the "constitutional questions." In fact, however, it is more likely to be based on the early learning of an intense affective opinion, and bolstered by the subsequent cognitive elaboration.

On face value, then, much public opinion would seem to be basically "irrational" in nature. It is to this question of "rationality" that we now turn.

71

The Problem
of
Rationality

Definition of Rationality

There is little sense in the global question, Is man
irrational? Since all men are mixtures of rationality and irrationality,
the important questions are: Under what circumstances are men
more rational? Which men, under these circumstances, are
more rational than others? But to deal
with "rationality" we must see how it will be used.
In the political sphere, what constitutes a "rational" citizen?

A man who behaves rationally is open to new information, no matter whether it comforts or pains him. This means that he must actively seek information which is pertinent to the issues of the day, and it means that he must not seek only that which is compatible with his own prejudices. The rational person, then, attempts to formulate an opinion on the basis of the best information available, selecting primarily on the basis of reliability and relevance.

However, it is not enough merely to be exposed to diverse sources of information. A rational man can perceive without distortion and remember accurately even information which radically disagrees with his own opinions or runs counter to his own thinking. He does not simply attend to those parts of arguments which are consonant with his beliefs nor remember only that which bolsters his prejudices. In short, to be rational a man must expose himself to congenial and uncongenial matters alike; he must be able to look at both and perceive them as they are, not merely as what he would like them to be, and he must be able to retain this information in undistorted form.

When processing information to which he has been exposed, a rational man must again resist pressures to minimize inconsistency. For example, he must be able to distinguish the worth of an argument from the palatability of its source. He must resist the temptation to distort an argument to fit into a prearranged category or stereotype. He must also avoid compartmentalizing his thinking—his thoughts must have access to one another. The capacity for logical inference is important in this connection; a supporter of an aggressive foreign policy must be able to make the appropriate logical inferences about the required size of the military budget. To make such inferences, the rational man clearly needs to be able to tolerate the possible consequences; if it leads him to the discovery that two of his opinions are inconsistent with one another, he must be prepared to face that fact. One unhappy consequence of the lack of policy responsibilities delegated to the average citizen is that he can easily, in his opinions, indulge in wishful thinking without practical regard for the possible incompatibility of wished-for outcomes.

Thus in processing incoming information, the rational man must be able to tolerate and perceive inconsistencies, to tolerate a certain amount of dissonance-arousal. At the same time, he cannot be a mere *tabula rasa*. He must have a capacity for critical reality-testing. When an argument is presented to him, he must meet it with a kind of censoring device which gauges the ideas against his previous experience and the experience of others whom he trusts. In other words, he must be able to assess the plausibility of the information he receives. In the case of the "Invasion from Mars" to be discussed below, we shall see how important this sense of reality can be.

73

In the preceding chapter we described the effects upon cognition of a radical and swift affective change toward an opinion object. Emotion and logic must be combined, in the rational man's opinions, in some kind of balance. The indignant citizen often manipulates his cognitions in the service of some compelling emotional need, such as an embracing hostility toward authority. Insofar as he merely uses arguments to rationalize his indignation, he is not thinking rationally. On the other hand, the rational citizen must in fact be able to relate incoming information to personal interests about which he feels deeply. The individual who forms opinions in ignorance of his short-term and long-term personal interests is not acting rationally either.

From this it must be clear that a final, and crucial, component of rationality must be awareness of one's own motives. When someone hates another man, he must be aware that he indeed does hate him, and not, as many do, protest his affection for him, or rationalize the personal antipathy as reflecting an ideological dispute. A legislator may be rational if he opposes a bill as a favor to special economic interests in his constituency, even if publicly he rationalizes his opposition as reflecting some grand principle of political ideology. He is not rational, however, if he fools himself, under such circumstances, into thinking that his vote is primarily motivated by adherence to some such doctrine.

Clearly, then, a rational man must be able to tolerate a moderate degree of inconsistency in his opinions and in his values. Only in the most extreme ideologies are all opinions and "facts" entirely consistent with one another. The press of the real world is such that one cannot always entirely reconcile, for example, a desire for peace and a desire for furtherance of the national interest, or a belief that all men should be treated equally and a belief that certain people should be given a slightly better than even break (the physically handicapped, for example, or members of minority groups that are discriminated against). The mark of a rational man, then, is that he knows when to balance one value or personal interest off against another and maximizes consistency of his actions with the whole panoply of his values, beliefs, and interests.

Rationality and Opinion Formation

As we indicated in the last chapter, the ways in which many opinions are formed violate these prescriptions for rationality. Most opinions seem to be formed from social referents; parents serve as referents for the child, and later on, group norms seem to guide many citizens toward the formulation of opinions on unfamiliar issues. These referents do not ordinarily reflect an adequate or unbiased sampling of the informational environment. Opinions are often learned as mere affective tendencies, as "pro" or "con" feelings, without adequate informational support. They are formed on the basis of biased exposure to information, and selective perception and selective learning. Contradictory information is often ignored, even when the citizen permits himself to become aware of its existence. Information which

74

bolsters an already firm opinion is accepted, very often regardless of the reliability of its source; an argument from a disliked source is often rejected out of hand, without adequate consideration of its merits. All the while, the simple affective tendencies learned in childhood or from group norms are cognitively elaborated and rationalized, occasionally into full-blown ideologies; the citizen often thinks that he is accepting information because of its intellectual merits, whereas in actuality the reason frequently has much more to do with its compatibility with the unconsidered premises of childhood. Logic is exploited in the service of defending these simple affective tendencies, rather than guiding an honest search for some "truth" which can be independently validated. Knowledge is compartmentalized when it is not convenient to relate incompatible truths. In short, most citizens are not, by these standards, notably "rational" in their political thinking. Their main interest lies in defending emotionally derived and poorly considered opinions—opinions based on early imitation of parental beliefs, partisan adherence to the norms of various groups, and selfish economic or personal interests.

However, these patterns of opinion formation and response to information are, like all social science laws, merely tendencies or probabilities; they do not operate uniformly in all individuals, nor in all situations, nor on all topics.

"Rational" Issues and "Irrational" Issues

Let us then turn first to the differences in political issues which highlight differences in the "rationality" of the electorate. Which issues seem to "pull" irrational responses the most? Let us remember, as we do so, that these are speculative comments generally unsupported by the research which characterizes most of our other statements.

Politics is a field which embraces a variety of topics. On the one hand, as Harold Lasswell says, "Politics is the process by which the irrational bases of society are brought out into the open."[1] But, on the other hand, it is also the sphere where, in a calculated and wholly rational fashion, men may pursue advantages denied to them by the marketplace or available only through political channels; patronage is the most obvious of these.

Something of this distinction between "irrational" topics and "rational" topics is embraced in the concepts of "style" issues compared with "position" issues put forward by Berelson, Lazarsfeld, and McPhee. The style issue (such as compulsory prayers in public schools) is largely self-expressive, rather than based on a more direct self-interest (for example, minimum wage law); it deals typically with matters of taste and manner of life rather than material gain; its basis is likely to be religious or ethnic or cultural grouping rather than occupational or socio-economic status; it is shorter in historical duration, and it provides more indirect gratifications,

[1] Harold D. Lasswell, *Psychopathology and Politics,* reprinted in *The Political Writings of Harold Lasswell* (New York: The Free Press of Glencoe, 1951), p. 184.

such as the success of some admired cause, compared with the direct and tangible gratifications going to the winner on a position issue.[2]

If one had to make the choice, one would say that style issues would, in the sense we have described, be a more likely target for irrational thought. But this is misleading, because an individual may be quite rational in his thinking about, say, prohibition, and quite irrational or fetishistic in his thinking about money. There is a better way to uncover the kinds of topics which invite irrational thought. Here are a few criteria: The (a) more vague the referents of an opinion, (b) more remote and difficult to assess its action consequences, and (c) more abstract the terms of debate, the more likely it is to invite irrational thinking. Thus, foreign policy will invite more irrational comment than will policy on minimum wages.

Topics dealing with material commonly repressed by individuals are also likely to invite irrational opinion. Obvious examples are war or criminal punishment (both dealing with aggression) and birth control or obscenity legislation (both dealing with sexuality). Socially "dangerous" topics, such as communism and religion, also draw a host of irrational defensive maneuvers. The social "dangers" they represent frequently parallel unconscious intra-physic "dangers." For example, an individual with a strong unconscious hatred for all authority may see in Soviet communism a system which threatens intrusion of authoritarian demands into every area of his life. His anti-communism may thus stem more from a residual hatred for his father than from any rational assessment of its likely effects on his life.

Opinions dealing with people (such as political candidates) or social groups (such as "bureaucrats," "blue bloods," or the various ethnic groups), are more likely to invite irrational thought than opinions dealing with most domestic economic issues. Few people can give as clear an account of why they like a man as why they like an economic policy; the "warm"-"cold" dimension seems crucial in many "person perception" studies, but the grounds for "warm" or "cold" feelings are usually obscure.[3] Studies of ethnic prejudice and social distance reveal the inaccessibility of many such opinions to new evidence; they are often compartmentalized, and usually rationalized; that is, covered by a plausible explanation which an impartial student of the opinion is inclined to discount.

The invitation to irrational thought may be, and often is, resisted, of course, yet it seems probable that these kinds of political topics encourage irrational thinking more than others.

Individual Differences in Rationality

Who will accept this invitation when others do not? Where will he be found? There are two factors which encourage rationality and discourage its opposite—education and mental health. Education teaches logical

[2] Bernard R. Berelson, Paul F. Lazarsfeld, and William N. McPhee, *Voting* (Chicago: University of Chicago Press, 1954), p. 184.

[3] Harold H. Kelley, "The Warm-Cold Variable in First Impressions of Persons," *Journal of Personality*, Vol. 18 (1950), pp. 431–439.

The Problem of Rationality

thought, shows men how to move from the concrete to the abstract level with some control, teaches the handling of evidence and the value of realistic perception, encourages, to some extent, the controlled flexibility of ideas, makes mental effort easier. Mental health implies self-acceptance, hence less need to project one's unacceptable feelings onto others, greater psychic energy available for reality testing, less obsessive and rigid thought patterns, a balance between immediate emotional release and the pursuit of some more distant goal, and other conditions conducive to rationality.

We know the general prevalence in our society of higher education: it is associated with higher occupational status, particularly professional work; it is higher in urban areas than rural areas, higher among the young than the old (due to the rising educational standards in the post-war years), higher among whites than non-whites, higher in the non-South than the South. Among the educated, urban, young, white groups, then, we would expect greater rationality, albeit a rationality in every case heavily larded with rationalization and marked by a self-interest which prevents these groups from serving as the "guardians" Plato envisioned for the ideal society. Government in the interest of any particular class is not what we want, in any case, whether they are highly educated or not. But what about the prevalence of mental health in society? This is harder to discover, although recent research gives us some clues.

The best recent study of the prevalence of impairment of mental health, conducted by a team of psychiatrists and sociologists, examined a random sample of 1,660 residents in midtown Manhattan, giving each respondent a private intensive interview designed to assess impairment of emotional and cognitive processes, inter-personal maladjustment, somatic symptoms and conversions, and other psychic impairments.[4] By the authors' criteria, about a fifth of the population was wholly free of any important symptoms of disturbance, a little over a half had mild to moderate symptoms, and about a quarter were more seriously impaired in their daily functioning. Briefly, this study found the following tendencies in the distribution of impaired mental health:

1. It was least prevalent among the young adults (20–29) and most prevalent among the oldest age group studied (50–59).

2. There were no important differences between married men and married women, but unmarried men were more likely to have impaired mental health than unmarried women. (The authors discuss and reject the idea that this was due to the particular selection of people living in mid-Manhattan.)

3. Generation time (whether a person is born abroad, is the child of immigrants, or the grandchild of immigrants, etc.) was not clearly related to mental health. However, among first or second generation Americans, the type of community he or his parents came from made a difference. Those from foreign rural and village backgrounds suffered higher rates of impairment than those from foreign urban backgrounds.

4. For our purposes, the most important relationship has to do with

[4] Leo Srole and others, *Mental Health in the Metropolis, The Midtown Manhattan Study* (New York: McGraw-Hill, 1962).

77

The Problem of Rationality

socio-economic status. There was an overwhelmingly strong relationship between the socio-economic status or class of one's parents and the probability of psychic impairment—the better off one's parents were, the healthier one is likely to be. This is also true of one's own status, although it is harder to disentangle cause and effect in this respect (since people with impaired mental functioning decline in the status ladder of occupations, while those with better mental health rise to higher status). The prevalence of the various types of impairments, however, were not equally related to status; some, like anxiety, tension, and overindulgence (excessive intake—coffee, liquor, smoking) were equally prevalent in the children of all status groups. But among the impairments which were more prevalent in the lower-status groups, two are especially significant for our interests: a hostile suspiciousness toward other people, the ideal milieu for paranoid opinions and a tendency to impute one's own "bad" impulses to others; and "rigidity," the foundation for compartmentalized thinking, selective and self-serving perception.

Of course, the study of people from midtown Manhattan will not tell us much about rural-urban differences—except that people who come to Manhattan from small American towns have *less* psychic impairment than those born and brought up there. It is possible, however, that such immigrants were among the most vigorous and healthy residents of those small towns, so it is difficult to draw a firm conclusion from this finding.

We have reviewed these matters at some length, because they shed light on both the prevalence and the origins of irrationality in opinion formation, at least to the extent that a general psychic impairment or anxiety are reflected in particular areas of thought. Following up these insights and interpolating with other information in these studies we may say that the social circumstances inhibiting rationality are as follows:[5]

The stresses of low status, poverty, and inadequate tools for coping with the demands of everyday life.

The stresses of culture shock: immigrating from a peasant culture to a foreign urban culture (reflected in differential impairment of European immigrants according to the ruralness of their places of origin and in the very high rate of impairment of Puerto Ricans).

The stresses occasioned by abrupt changes in family situation (the arrival of children and the departure of grown children).

The stresses of certain kinds of isolation (a cause and symptom as well as an effect) as evidenced in the higher impairment of the unmarried and the divorced of both sexes.

The Historical Moment and Irrationality

History is an important component in the development of irrational thinking on a given topic. When a particular issue is much in the forefront of public attention, it is considerably more likely to draw irrational opinions.

[5] Of course this does not purport to be a complete account of the etiology of mental disease; only a few of the main findings on broad social patterns affecting mental health can be mentioned here.

The Problem of Rationality

In the summer of 1963, the Negro issue was just such a salient issue; desegregation of the University of Alabama, demonstrations against discriminatory employment throughout the nation, demonstrations against housing and school discrimination in various cities of the North, and the introduction of civil rights legislation in Congress—all of these contributed to a rather sudden rise in attention to the issue of racial discrimination. This was illustrated by the sharp increase, from April to July, in the "racial problem" response to the Gallup Poll question "What do you think is the most important problem facing this country today?" In April only 4 per cent made such a response, while in July 49 per cent did so.

AN INVASION FROM MARS

The imminence of war, or threats of war, frequently provide the historical circumstances for inducing irrational thinking on related issues. An excellent example of this is the panic occasioned by "an invasion from Mars."[6] On the evening of October 30, 1938, Orson Welles and the Mercury Theater broadcast a radio version of H. G. Wells' *War of the Worlds* over the Columbia network. The script, cast in the style of a news broadcast, "reported" the arrival of a strange cylindrical meteor in mid-Jersey, the emergence from the meteor of Martian monsters, a battle between national guard units and the Martians, the victory of the Martians due to their superior weapons, the spreading out of the area controlled by the Martians, with place names mentioned, something of the life under Martian rule, and the final victory over the Martians—not by man but by microbes and diseases. The response to this broadcast can best be described by a few reports of individuals who panicked upon hearing the broadcast:

I was terribly frightened. I wanted to pack and take my child in my arms, gather up my friends and get in the car and just go north as far as we could. But what I did was just set by one window, prayin', listenin', and scared stiff and my husband by the other snifflin' and lookin' out to see if people were runnin'.

I held a crucifix in my hand and prayed while looking out of my open window for falling meteors.

I ran downstairs to the telephone and called my mother. She hadn't been listening. Then I took the little baby and my husband wrapped our seven-year old child and we rode with friends who live on the street to the tavern where my mother works.

I ran out of the house. I guess I didn't know what I was doing. I stood on the corner waiting for a bus and I thought every car that came along was a bus and I ran out to get it. People saw how excited I was and tried to quiet me, but I kept saying over and over again to everybody I met: 'Don't you know New Jersey is destroyed by the Germans—it's on the radio.'

Why should these people have behaved as they did? All they had to do was turn the dial and see what was on other stations, or look at the

6 The following account is taken from Hadley Cantril, Hazel Gaudet, and Herta Herzog, *The Invasion from Mars* (Princeton: Princeton University Press, 1940).

The Problem of Rationality

paper to see that *The War of the Worlds* was scheduled for that time, or examine the internal evidence in the broadcast to test its plausibility. Most of the listeners did these things, but a very substantial part of the population responded irrationally, as we have seen. Who were they and why did they lose their sense of reality?

Cantril, in analyzing interview data on 135 persons, most of whom were upset by the broadcast, concluded that lack of critical ability was the key factor in the panic. Critical ability was, as might be expected, associated with education attainment, but even among those of low education who were not panicked, there was evidence of a kind of habit of reading and self-education which may have been important.

But, of course, no such general demographic characteristic can account for personal behavior of the kind described above. The phenomena were more complex. What are the personal characteristics associated with a highly suggestible frame of mind when faced by a situation interpreted as dangerous? Cantril finds the following kinds of things relevant:[7]

1. Insecurity and worry. Those who panicked seemed, more than others, to have a series of worries about their jobs, their looks, their acceptability to others. 'My husband, for the last ten years has had no steady work.' 'I'm so worried about my looks. It's time I was getting married but the boys I like never like me.' 'As you see I'm a colored man. I can't get as good a job as I think I deserve.'

2. Phobias. 'I lived through an earthquake in Austria and explosions of any kind scare me.' 'Twenty years ago I saw lightning strike the ocean and divide the water. I felt it came from heaven and this broadcast reported things just like that.'

3. Lack of self-confidence. People who panicked were more likely to say that in arguments with respected persons they preferred to conciliate their opponent than to maintain their own point of view.

4. Fatalistic. 'When the time comes you go and there is no getting away from it.' 'I believe that what is to be will be.' 'God had put us on this earth for his honor and glory and that it was for Him to say when it was our time to go.'

5. Religiosity and frequency of church attendance. 'We just sat and listened. You see we're good Christians and a Providence will take care of us.' 'The Bible says that the first time the end of the world was by flood and the next time it will be fire and that went through my mind.'

More generally, it appeared that the intellectual frame of reference was an important influencing factor. Like the reactionary who will believe anything bad about a liberal or the communist who will believe anything good about the Soviet Union, the person who expected strange and improbable events, either as "Acts of God" or in some other guise, was more ready to accept the invasion from Mars as news rather than as a piece of fiction. People already prepared for a "second coming" or a judgment day or sudden destruction were not as disposed to check the facts because the invasion of the Martians was plausible on the face of it.

We said that rationality included an acceptance of one's emotional

[7] *Ibid.*, pp. 132–134.

The Problem of Rationality

life; the phobias of these panicking people were evidence of internal conflicts involving repressed emotions. Selective perception in the service of some preconceived beliefs, is, we said, at war with rationality. Here those people with preconceived notions of imminent destruction, who selected only such evidence as supported this belief, were those who panicked. The capacity for critical reality-testing is a feature of the more rational mind; this was exactly what was lacking among the poor panicking New Jersey citizens of 1938. And, if these qualities were combined with worry, lack of self-confidence, fatalism, and religiosity, the result was something which, although in this instance turned out to be more ridiculous than tragic, might, in another "emergency" be disastrous.

Finally, it is worthwhile to describe the historical and social background which contributed to the plausibility of the broadcast as news. The time was the second quarter of the twentieth century, when a variety of social norms were in flux and the certainty as to what was believable and what unbelievable eroded by rapid social change. The specific decade was one of great personal insecurity; many of those who had believed the broadcast had experienced periods of unemployment which had been unsettling. Just as other attitudes are generalized, so too are attitudes or moods of insecurity, anxiety, even panic. Specifically, the broadcast followed by only five months the Munich war scare which had received widespread radio coverage and had been experienced in an atmosphere of the possibility of imminent disaster. History, so to speak, had prepared people for panic.

Rationality and Group Reference

One of the recurring themes of this little book is the degree to which men adopt opinions by "referring" the matter to some group loyalty: ethnic, occupational, trade union, or perhaps such vague referents as "the common man" (as when people are for the Democratic party because it is "the party of the common man"). Such group reference serves to orient people in the absence of much other information or attention to the matter at hand. Indeed, public affairs are so peripheral to most persons' lives, and so seemingly remote in their consequences, that some such orientation is necessary if opinions are to be formulated at all.

In this context, group reference would appear to have a further function; it may make the process of translating complex pieces of information into public opinion more "rational" than is the case when individuals are left to their own rather irrational thought processes. That is, opinions formed by this group reference may tend to reflect longer range, more salient individual interests than opinions formed in the absence of group reference.

There are, of course, limits to the rationality of group reference. Individuals who have no "self" other than their "group self" and no individuality or independence are not likely to be more rational. In the midtown Manhattan study, members of ethnic groups who identified most closely with their groups had *higher* rates of impairment than did the more detached ethnic group members, although this was partly due to various other factors affecting this population identifying with its ethnic groups.[8] Group reference is certainly no panacea. Moreover, there are times when entire groups (and not just mobs or crowds), even entire nations, lose their rationality. G. M. Gilbert, on the basis of his experience with the Nazi leaders at the Nuremburg trials and a more general study of the Nazi movement, describes this as "cultural pseudopathology." The term refers to a situation where the individuals may use the reality testing procedures of their culture, but these procedures may themselves be strained toward certain irrational beliefs. In such a culture men may "have developed, from earliest childhood, attitudes of persecution, superiority, special revelation, or manifest destiny to rule the world as a national consequence of ethnic identification and indoctrination. [In this way] the possibility of reality-testing has simply been artificially limited by the nature of the cultural learning process."[9] With this in mind, and the case of the invasion from Mars before us, we must add to the circumstances which discourage rationality among individuals a historical factor and a cultural factor. Historically, popular rationality seems to be reduced by the great traumas of war and depression. Culturally, it is affected by the mythological foundations of social thought: racial superiority, dialectical materialism, belief in the guiding presence of an "unseen hand." These instances of irrationally behaving groups underscore, of course, the necessity for rational group leaders.

But, once again, granted the limits and distortions of group and national reference, it is often true that the pathologies of human thought may be reduced by group reference and filtered through group leadership, so that a more rational product ensues. Among other things, group discussion is a means to this greater rationality.

Is this just another word for conformity? We turn to this problem in the next section.

[8] Srole and others, *op. cit.*, pp. 285–289.
[9] G. M. Gilbert, *The Psychology of Dictatorship* (New York: Ronald, 1950), pp. 270–271.

The Problem of Rationality

The Problem of of Conformity

Reviewing the literature of social criticism
from 1949 to 1958, Winston White finds
that the one most consistent theme has been the fear of
and attack upon "conformity."[1] Much of this seems to take off
from Riesman's idea of the changing
American character, the shift from conscience
as a source of guidance in the 19th century to peer groups

[1] Winston White, *Beyond Conformity* (New York: The Free Press of
Glencoe, 1961) p. 16. I am indebted to White for suggesting
several ideas in the following analysis.

as a source of guidance now. Riesman refers to this as a movement from "inner-direction" to "other-direction." "What is common to all other-directeds," he says, "is that their contemporaries are the source of direction for the individual—either those known to him or those with whom he is indirectly acquainted, through friends and through the mass media. . . . The goals for which the other-directed person strives shift . . . it is only the process of striving itself and the process of paying close attention to the signals from others that remain unaltered throughout life."[2] This is similar to Erich Fromm's view that modern society has developed the "marketing personality," of which the main theme is the way man experiences himself and others: "the experience of oneself as a commodity and of one's value as exchange value." To be a success "as a commodity" in a changing market one must be an empty vessel into which one can "pour in the right trait at the right time."[3] Again, the conformist theme; and beyond that, the perception of an undifferentiated and undistinguished society marked by a drab sameness of literature, art, politics, and people.

There was enough in what we saw of processes of opinion formation and change to give some plausibility to this criticism. In primary groups, experiments have shown that men may be quickly led to perceive objects and people and issues as the other group members do. For example, if a person gives an opinion on, say, Soviet Russia, in private, and later learns that the group opinion is different, the chances are about fifty-fifty that he will modify his opinion toward the group norm.[4] And if the power of face-to-face groups is great, so is the influence of reference groups as sources of opinion and standards of behavior. Both social critics and working psychologists seem to be talking about the same thing. But when research attention focuses more directly on conformity and other-directedness, one finds that people must be talking about somewhat different things. Let us examine three interpretations of other-direction.

1. *Other-directedness (field dependence) and the passive self.* Elaine Graham Sofer developed an "inner-directed vs. other-directed questionnaire . . . designed to evaluate the relative importance for a person of personal goals and standards as opposed to conformity and adaptation to the group."[5] She found that the other-directeds were more likely than others to change their opinions when presented with an authoritative statement contrary to their expressed beliefs. Moreover, there were a variety of personality correlates which suggested a broader pattern of passivity and dependence upon the environment for guidance (field dependence). Of these two elements (weak self and strong sense of environment) Mrs. Sofer says, "our over-all findings indicate that the pattern of other-direction is far more

[2] David Riesman, *The Lonely Crowd* (New Haven, Yale University Press, 1950), p. 22.

[3] Erich Fromm, *Man for Himself* (New York: Rinehart, 1947), pp. 68, 76.

[4] Raymond L. Gorden, "Interaction Between Attitude and the Definition of the Situation in the Expression of Opinion," *American Sociological Review*, Vol. 17 (1952), pp. 50–58.

[5] Harriet Linton and Elaine Graham (Sofer), "Personality Correlates of Persuasibility," in C. I. Hovland, and I. L. Janis (eds.), *Personality and Persuasibility* (New Haven: Yale University Press, 1959), p. 70.

The Problem of Conformity

likely to be based upon a weak, passive self-image, and the inhibition of inner awareness, than upon any special sensitivity toward the environment or upon positive response tendencies toward other people."[6]

2. *Other-directedness and freedom from institutional pressures.* Contrast this with McClelland's view of other-directedness. After examining some measures of the contents of children's stories in a variety of countries and extracting from them inferences on social character, he says " 'Other-directedness,' more or less in Riesman's sense of the term, seems to be correlated with rapid economic development."[7] Obviously McClelland does not mean that weak and passive persons who are acted upon by the environment but do not initiate action themselves, stimulate economic growth. An examination of his measure of "other-directedness" shows the difference. He examines the incidents and themes in stories taken from children's readers in some 41 countries around the world to see the nature of the pressures to which the characters in these stories are responding. Basically he assumes that "an other directed society should be one in which ego [the hero of the story] is not motivated to interact by traditional institutional pressures [the church or the government tells him to do something] but by pressures from others, particularly peers, whose demands are respected enough to produce compliance."[8] This implies a different kind of conformity, based upon respect for public opinion rather than for tradition or social institutions. It says nothing about the giving up of one's personal goals.

3. *Other-directedness combined with internalized norms.* A way out of this dilemma is suggested by a further piece of research following up Riesman's ideas of the conflict between internalized goals and a high value placed upon peer approval. Inquiring into the nature of adolescent values, Riley, Riley, and Moore, asked some 2,500 American high school students to respond to a set of "vignettes" of different kinds of student models ("Paul and Miriam are good students. Although they are not bookworms or grinds, they get good marks because they spend quite a bit of time studying and are always on the beam when it comes to their work."). The high school students were asked whether they wanted to be like "Paul and Miriam," whether the well-liked kids in their classes want their friends to be like them, and so forth. What these authors found was that although there were a number of students who chose a clear "other-directed" pattern of vignette models there were no pure "inner-directed" achievement-oriented students. All those who revealed a set of internalized goals were also eager to have peer group approval; that is, "they expect to follow their consciences and to be approved by their peers in addition. Thus their predominant inner-directedness emerges only when they are forced, through a conflict situation, to separate internalized norms from peer-group ap-

[6] Elaine Graham Sofer, "Inner-Direction, Other-Direction, and Autonomy: A Study of College Students," in Seymour M. Lipset and Leo Lowenthal (eds.), *Culture and Social Character* (New York: The Free Press of Glencoe, 1961), p. 339.

[7] David C. McClelland, *The Achieveing Society* (Princeton: Van Nostrand, 1961), p. 187.

[8] *Ibid.*, p. 198. It should be observed that McClelland's idea of "other-directedness" is very different from his n-affiliation, with which it might be confused.

85

The Problem of Conformity

proval."[9] It was this forced choice, then, which gave Mrs. Sofer a group of rather passive "pure" other-directeds revealing the lack of internalized norms and the low self-esteem of the persuasible person. Where this is not the case, the "inner-and-other directed" persons ". . . seem to take for granted that their own goals and their desire for approval from others, far from conflicting with one another, tend to fit together."[10] From Mc-Clelland's discussion, we can assume that he is speaking of just such "inner-*and*-other direction"—not the persuasible, passive, field-dependent, purely other-directed type—since his contrast is not between inner- and other-direction, but rather between the third of Riesman's trilogy, tradition-direction, and, as it now appears, the combination of the other two.

The truth of the matter seems to be that in modern society the "opposite" of the pure other-directed individual is not the inner-directed (field independent) person, but the person, so far un-named, who reacts negatively to public opinion and to attempts of others to persuade him. Although there is some ambiguity in this matter, it seems generally true that the unpersuadible person, the extreme nonconformist, is hostile and anxious, or possibly withdrawn, and resists the cues of public opinion less often because of internalized norms and more often because of personality difficulties.[11]

The American Pattern: Sensitivity to Others and Obligations to Self

This particular pattern of inner-and-other directedness, sensitivity to group opinion fortified by inner values, seems to be learned in a special way. Testing sensitivity to public opinion, McClelland finds that Americans, more than Germans, agree to such items as "the negative opinion of others often keeps me from seeing a movie or a play I had planned to attend," or "my political opinion is easily swayed by editorials I read." Going beyond this into how this other-directedness is learned, in a study of German and American boys of high school age, he found that although the American boys engaged in far more group activities, compared with the more solitary activities of the Germans (walking, collecting stamps, playing music), the German value structure emphasized duty to others much more than the Americans, who emphasized such personal values as "to be intelligent, to appreciate music, to enjoy life. . . . So, while the German engages in more individualistic activities, he has a great sense of his obligation to others, whereas the American has a greater obligation to himself which is held in check by participation in many group activities."[12] This nicely illustrates another strand in the interwoven pattern of atten-

[9] Matilda White Riley, John W. Riley, Jr., and Mary E. Moore, "Adolescent Values and the Riesman Typology: An Empirical Analysis," in Lipset and Lowenthal, *op. cit.*, p. 382.
[10] *Ibid.*, p. 385.
[11] See I. L. Janis, "Personality Correlates of Susceptibility to Persuasion," *Journal of Personality*, Vol. 4 (1954), pp. 504–518; I. L. Janis and Donald Rife, "Persuasibility and Emotional Disorder," in Hovland and Janis, *op. cit.*, pp. 121–137.
[12] McClelland, *op. cit.*, pp. 197–198.

The Problem of Conformity

tion to self and respect for the opinions of others. The pure other-directed (in the sense of Sofer ID-OD scale) would be a high group participant and a person with few self-referential values. On every measure, McClelland finds Americans, compared with people in other cultures, to be especially sensitive to public opinion, and generally more other-directed.

To summarize this discussion, then, we have found at least three views of other-directedness, each discovered and measured in empirical studies. The first describes the passive, field-dependent person who relies wholly on others for orientation and guidance. But this seems to have been partly a product of the measures used to isolate such a person—although he does exist. The second describes the person who substitutes public opinion for institutional or traditional norms as the source of his orientation. Perhaps the key to the change implied in this substitution is the use of a more flexible source of guidance, one more open to the needs of new historical situations. The third, then, describes the person with a respect for public opinion, not as a substitute for internalized values, but rather combined with them. Openness to the suggestions of public opinion comes, in this view, from a respect for others combined with a respect for oneself. And, in McClelland's study, it appears that this latter syndrome is learned and expressed in a distinctive American pattern: high social participation with a sense of obligation to the self.

Yet all of these views have one element in common: individual guidance by group opinion; that is, a tendency toward conformity. Here is where the criticism of modern man which Winston White found so prevalent in what he calls the "ideology of the intellectuals" comes to a common focus. To remind us again of this theme, we will quote White:

Whenever the individual finds himself in a group, our commentators tell us, be it in the office or over the barbecue pit, he wants to fit in and be accepted; like Willy Loman, he wants not only to be liked but to be well-liked. He strives for this by being sensitive to what the rest of the group considers acceptable standards of behavior (other direction) and acts accordingly; in short, he conforms. Since in conformity, he is careful not to do or say anything that will rub the *others* the wrong way, the idiosyncratic rough edges of *his* personality are rubbed away; in consequence, he becomes scarcely distinguishable from those whose approbation he seeks.[13]

The Social Implications of Conformity

Keeping in mind this criticism, and not forgetting the various uses of the term "conformity" and "other direction," let us examine how the same behavior may either be condemned as socially dangerous, or, viewed from another standpoint, may be appreciated as socially useful. And this ambivalence *may* be justified whether or not the individuals involved have, in fact, a set of internalized norms which guide them in difficult situations. What follows then, is a brief consideration of twelve criticisms of conformist behavior commonly leveled against "modern man," or "mass man."

Bandwagon appeal. It has been argued that Americans, more than

13 White, *op. cit.*, p. 16.

others, want to associate themselves with majority electoral opinion because it bears the stamp of "being right." In support of this position, Lazarsfeld's study of Erie County voters showed that a few, at least, demonstrated receptivity to the bandwagon appeal. Lazarsfeld demonstrated this as follows. *All* those who did not know who they were going to vote for in May but who knew which party they thought would win (21 cases), eventually voted for the party they thought would win, thus suggesting (but not proving) the power of expectation on voting decision. This is coupled with such statements as the following:

> Just before the election it looked like Roosevelt would win so I went with the crowd. Didn't make any difference to me who won but *I wanted to vote for the winner*.

> I have always been a Democrat, but lately I've heard of so many Democrats who are going to vote Republican that *I might do the same*. Four out of five Democrats that I know are doing that.[14]

Further analysis shows that although projection of one's own latent voting intention onto others may have accounted for some of the correspondence of expectation with vote decision, this could not have explained most of this relationship. Furthermore, "public opinion polls as a source of change in expectation were explicitly mentioned by forty-two respondents."[15]

Because arguments about the bandwagon appeal have been used to criticize the social value of the pre-election public opinion polls, George Gallup made a study to see if he could detect it. He found no difference in the opinions of those who knew the poll results and those who did not, and furthermore, argued that the fact of a declining majority in successive pre-election polls showed at least the weakness, if not the absence, of the bandwagon appeal.[16] Nevertheless, the Lazarsfeld and associates findings are the more persuasive and are supported by a variety of other evidence showing popular accommodation to what they perceive to be the mode in some relevant public. Is it such a bad thing?

Consider the problem of accommodating to the victory of the "other party" and the "opposing candidate" after an election. Americans who voted against the winner tend to change their opinions of the victorious group so as to make it possible for them to support him. They find him a better person than they thought he was during the campaign and his policies less damaging. After a little while some will "remember" having voted for him. The desire to be part of the mainstream of public opinion provides, for a while, social support for the new incumbent, and although it erodes quickly, is useful in facilitating political changeover.

Uniformity of opinion and behavior. As noted above, many of the critics of society find the tendency to conform in dress, taste, and political opinion a depressing phenomenon. They condemn it as vulgarization,

[14] Paul F. Lazarsfeld, Bernard R. Berelson, and Hazel Gaudet, *The People's Choice* (New York: Columbia University Press, 1948), p. 108.

[15] *Ibid.,* p. 109.

[16] George Gallup and Saul F. Rae, "Is There a Bandwagon Vote?" *Public Opinion Quarterly,* Vol. 4 (1940), pp. 244–249.

The Problem of Conformity

massification, or cultural homogenization. For them it represents the impoverishment of society. On the other hand, it may be viewed as routinizing a set of low-level instrumental choices so that the citizen is free to devote more time to things that concern him more. Winston White says, on this point, "the standards of certain patterns of behavior not essentially significant in human intercourse liberates the attention for more important considerations."[17] He quotes (of all people) William H. Whyte, the author of *The Organization Man*, as saying "surface uniformities can serve quite well as protective coloration . . . a sensible awareness of the rules of the game can be a condition of individualism as well as a constraint upon it."[18] Indeed, the conservation of time and energy is a major function of *selective* conformity, with its attendant uniformity of behavior.

Group productivity. Clearly, if everyone sought to maximize his agreement with others and his agreeableness in their eyes, group discussion would be fruitless. Who would perform the role of critic? Who would innovate? Who would bear the burden of (perhaps temporary) opprobrium in disciplining discussion and forcing the issue? There has been much unfavorable comment on the search for the "easiest" solution of a problem in American legislative halls—i.e., the solution which brings forth the least criticism, not the one that accomplishes the task in the best way. But, there is mounting evidence that every group is better off for a solidarity or group morale leader, as well as a task leader.[19] Furthermore, the presence of "popular" people in work groups tends to increase group effectiveness as does a general tendency toward "acceptance of others." However, "eccentricity" tends to decrease group effectiveness.

Anonymity. What the critics of conformity seem to fear is not so much that the "faces in the crowd" will turn mean or horrid but rather that they will disappear completely and we will be left only with the faceless crowd. In this they fear the ascendance of crowd psychology, mass man, anonymity. But, because of the plurality of groups and their crosscut pattern, one might equally argue that men achieve their individuality by their unique position in this group pattern. No two people share the same exact group affiliations (family, occupational group, friendship group, neighborhood); hence, by their efforts to identify with and somehow synthesize these group micro-cultures, each arrives not at faceless anonymity but rather at uniqueness and individuality, particularly in modern society.

Social criticism. On the one hand the very term conformity seems to imply the drastic reduction of social criticism. If a person conforms to social norms, how can he criticize these norms? But the same research which shows that people often seek the anonymity of a group and behave in a way which, as individuals alone they would find reprehensible (as,

17 White, *op. cit.*, pp. 154–155.
18 *Ibid.*, p. 155.
19 Philip E. Slater, "Role Differentiation," reprinted in A. Paul Hare, Edgar F. Borgatta, and Robert F. Bales (eds.), *Small Groups* (New York: Knopf, 1955), pp. 498–515.
20 William Haythorn, "The Influence of Individual Members on the Characteristics of Small Groups," *Journal of Abnormal and Social Psychology*, Vol. 48 (1953), pp. 276–284.

for example, Legionnaires might behave at a Legion Convention), also shows that such anonymity can lead men to express counter-norm criticism. Festinger, Pepitone, and Newcomb organized group discussions of attitudes toward parents following a statement about the high percentage of people who secretly had hostile feelings toward their mothers and fathers. Since there is a powerful social as well as psychological inhibition against expressing hostility toward parents, they believed that groups in which there was greater anonymity—that is, groups in which individuals could less easily be identified and their specific contributions to the discussion less clearly recalled—would be those in which a freer discussion of hostile attitudes toward parents would occur. As it turned out, their data confirmed their hypothesis. Moreover, those groups in which this anonymity occurred and in which the discussion became more free were those which, in retrospect, were more attractive to the members.[21] Losing oneself in a group, de-individuation, as the authors of this study term it, facilitates a kind of social criticism—and not necessarily an irresponsible one, either. Although in general the loss of restraint in groups is not so felicitous, at least it sometimes permits people to say critical things in a realistic way.

Ethical standards. On the one hand, groups seem to impose standards of behavior which are self-serving: unions become restrictionist, firms employ cartel adjustments. To the extent that individuals find their identity in groups they may lose a wider ethic with universal application. They may judge themselves wholly by in-group standards. On the other hand, groups may exercise restraint on the self-serving impulses of their members: the advertising council may, in deference to public criticism, upgrade the ethical standards of its members; professional standards are often in the public interest; the very idea of a group audience for individual conduct may help support a man's faltering superego.

Even in the case of the self-serving group standard, as with the rates of production well below the possible output established by factory work teams, the profile of the individualistic standard breaker or "rate buster" is not very favorable. He is a lone wolf in the factory and outside of it and often a person with strong upward mobility who "cuts himself off from others on the same level and seeks association with those of superior status."[22] In this latter case he may, indeed, not be much of an individualist with internalized standards, but rather a conformist with a reference status group of which he is not a member.

Identity. If a person loses himself in a group, so to speak, by adopting the group viewpoint and adding little of his own or if he has nothing to say until he finds out what is appropriate for a member of the group, he seems, from the outside, to have lost his identity. Yet it is the case that when people ask themselves the question "Who am I?" they tend first to identify themselves by social, rather than personal, references: by occupation, social and family status, nationality, religion, and where relevant, ethnic group as a

---

[21] Leon Festinger, A. Pepitone, and Theodore M. Newcomb, "Some Consequences of De-Individuation in a Group," *Journal of Abnormal and Social Psychology,* Vol. 47 (1952), pp. 382–389.

[22] William F. Whyte, *Money and Motivation* (New York: Harper, 1955), p. 42.

The Problem of Conformity

particularly salient feature. Those who skip this social identity and go directly to more personal characteristics are more likely to be disturbed.[23]

Freedom. In a traditional society, a *gemeinschaft* society, conformity to status, role, and group standards is the antithesis of objective freedom, though the individual may not experience the constraint. But in a society where individuals are likely to belong to many overlapping groups, with roles which make different and sometimes incompatible demands on loyalty and imply variant belief systems, the process of group reference and identification does not have this stultifying effect. In fact, if the essence of freedom is choice, such men, for all their tendencies toward conformity, are forced to be free. At times the burden of such choice is too great. McQuitty reports that among the mental patients he studied, there was evidence of selective and somewhat anarchic identification with "diverse categories of people."[24] Others have discovered a withdrawal pattern and generalized apathy for those who could not synthesize the belief systems of their various reference groups. But those who can selectively identify with selected aspects of several groups are, in fact, engaging in free choice.

Conservatism. Conformity to group standards reinforces the traditional patterns of thought (to be discussed below) because the group is the carrier of tradition (its own if no other), and it must change slowly, if at all, in order not to lose members; to the extent that it has leadership it has vested interests, organizational roots, routinized behavior—all of which are hard to change. It is this very quality of group-anchoredness of opinion, however, which keeps men from being easily manipulated by the passing persuasive stranger, and, paradoxically, by the politically conservative press.

But it is the premise that deserves closer examination: Is it true that men in groups are less psychologically mobile than men in isolation? The answer would be an extended one, scraping together pieces of evidence and differentiating situations and predispositions. But two clues suggest that group contact and empathy create mobility, for it seems to be the case, first, that men often exaggerate the force and extent of an opposing majority and hence are somewhat liberated by knowledge of its real nature,[25] and, second, that one true friend will enable a man to stand out against the hostile throng.[26] Moreover, in spite of Michels' alleged "iron law of oligarchy," which says that all political parties and organizations must become oligarchical, the leadership of parties and interest groups is more "open to experience" and alert to change, than most of the membership.

Empathy. The psychic device whereby men judge how others will

23 Muzafer Sherif, "The Self and Reference Groups: Meeting Ground of Individual and Group Approaches," *Annals of the New York Academy of Sciences*, Vol. 96 (1962), p. 802.

24 L. L. McQuitty, "A Measure of Personality Integration in Relation to the Concept of the Self," *Journal of Personality*, Vol. 18 (1950), p. 468.

25 See M. Brewster Smith, "The Personal Setting of Public Opinions: A Study of Attitudes Toward Russia," *Public Opinion Quarterly*, Vol. 11 (1947–48), pp. 522–523.

26 S. E. Asch, "Effects of Group Pressure Upon the Modification and Distortion of Judgments," in Dorwin Cartwright and Alvin Zander (eds.), *Group Dynamics* (Evanston, Ill.: Row, Peterson, 1953), pp. 151–162.

The Problem of Conformity

react to a given kind of behavior is empathy, putting themselves in the place of others. Perhaps in the process of exercising this faculty, they lose something of themselves, but they gain many "new selves" in the process. Moreover there is considerable evidence to suggest that this very faculty is one of the psychological foundations of a modern society. "Empathy," says Daniel Lerner, "is the capacity to see oneself in the other fellow's situation. This is an indispensable skill for people moving out of traditional settings. . . . In modern society *more* individuals exhibit *higher* emphathic capacity than in any previous society."[27] This empathy is learned through a practiced sensitivity to the thoughts and feelings of others.

Economic development. At an earlier point in this discussion we mentioned that McClelland claimed that other-directedness, in the sense of the absence of traditional pressures and the presence of sensitivity to public opinion, correlated with rapid economic development. In the stories told in children's readers, the emphasis upon institutional pressure for action (impersonal codes supplied by business, the church, the state, the schools, and so forth) was markedly *less* in the countries with economies currently growing more rapidly than others. Second, in those countries with more rapidly growing economies, the type of relationship among the characters in the stories seemed more "contractual," that is, men responded only because some specific motive was ascribed to them. This, it may be recalled, is part of the "shallow" type of inter-personal relations that Fromm finds particularly distasteful in modern "capitalist" society. Third, in the stories of the more rapidly developing economies "pressure for conformity came from 'peers' or 'the generalized other' " rather than "selfish" pursuit of individual gain. And this was equally true of both democratic and non-democratic nations. Finally, in the more rapidly developing countries, the stories were those where "the peer 'collectivity' or 'public opinion' more successfully forces the individual into line."[28] Taken all together these themes imply, as we have noted, a rejection of traditional or institutional codes and a sensitivity to the opinions of others: the other-directedness of Riesman's typology (with at least the possibility of retained internalized values, as well).

McClelland argues that this relationship of other-directedness to current economic development is based upon several factors. First, he says, this other-directed orientation promotes a shift from the remnants of old loyalties and norms to the more modern standards of organized public opinion as represented in the media. (The argument is somewhat faulty since the old norms are likely to be embodied in peer-group opinion—exactly the group Riesman thought controlled the other-directed man. But it does represent a partial break with the internalized norms of childhood; thus it is partially correct.) Second, McClelland holds that reliance on historic institutional codes means lack of flexibility compared with reliance on opinion susceptible to influence by the mass media. Finally, he says that the impersonal market requires the contractual, relatively shallow type of human relations influenced by shifting opinion to make it work, and a respect for

[27] Daniel Lerner, *The Passing of Traditional Society* (New York: The Free Press of Glencoe, 1958), pp. 50–51, Lerner's emphasis.
[28] McClelland, *op. cit.*, pp. 178–188.

The Problem of Conformity

the impersonal opinions of unknown others, in order to preserve quality of goods and services.[29] For these several reasons, all of which imply the value of sensitivity and respect for public opinion, as contrasted with traditions embodied in institutions and internalized moral codes, the modern economic system requires individuals to be conformist in this particular way—along with a high need to achieve. The combination of the two is important.

Political adaptability. The political system, like the economic system, needs a certain kind of conformist behavior. We saw this in connection with the bandwagon appeal, but it is true in another sense, as indicated by cross-national studies. Stanley Milgram recently studied the responses of French and Norwegian students (in their native countries) to the following situations. Each subject was placed in a listening booth situated among several similar booths and asked to discriminate between two tones, allegedly in order to improve communication to aircraft. On a set of headphones each heard other respondents, whom he believed to be in the adjoining booths, giving their reactions first, most of them perceptibly in error. On some of the trials, if the subject gave the correct answer, he heard snickers or comments suggesting he was showing off. Under all circumstances the Norwegians were more likely to follow the erroneous judgment of the group than the French; that is, they conformed more easily under all circumstances and responded with greater docility to the (unjustified) criticism of the others. For example, when exposed to the taunts of the group, the French subjects went along with the group on 59 per cent of the erroneous judgments—but the Norwegian subjects went along with the erroneous judgments 75 per cent of the time.[30]

One's first reaction, perhaps, is in praise of French individualism. Yet students of French government, such as Nathan Leites, Philip Converse, and Georges Dupeux, find that a persistent crippling defect among the French, both as legislators and individual citizens, is a combination of lack of group loyalty (particularly to one's political party) but also, in the legislature, to one's friends—a kind of self-centered reference for what is right and wrong.[31] One is one's own reference group. The consequence for France, as everyone knows, is not political adaptability, but immobilism. Some greater reliance on group reference, some greater trust in group judgment and leadership, some greater conformity, might well improve the French polity.

In some respects we are each of us alone. It is better that way. But in other respects, we must anchor our opinions in the opinions of the group, or better still, of many groups. At least we do well to listen to them.

[29] *Ibid.*, pp. 192–195.

[30] Stanley Milgram, "Nationality and Conformity," *Scientific American*, Vol. 205 (1961), pp. 45–51.

[31] Nathan Leites, *On the Game of Politics in France* (Stanford: Stanford University Press, 1959); Philip E. Converse and Georges Dupeux, "Politicization of the Electorate in France and the United States," *Public Opinion Quarterly*, Vol. 26 (1962), pp. 1–23.

The Problem of Conformity

The Problem

of

Intensity

The agency of change in society
is very often the social movement—religious, nationalist, communist,
racist, and nativist. Each has had its currency.
Sometimes even in the absence of a mass
movement, the zealot, the fanatic
with a single value and a single cause, stimulates
the society to change. The men of the mass
movements and the fanatics with a cause are, in Hoffer's term,
"True Believers," men with missions

94

framed in some more or less embracing ideology, seeking to redeem their lives and themselves through their apostolic actions.[1]

In distinction to the True Believer with his intense commitment, there is the Concerned Citizen, the man who is likely to register in the American surveys of public opinion as "very interested" in public affairs, who "personally cares a good deal about the outcome of elections," and who, "agrees strongly" or "disagrees strongly" with various proposed policies. Like the True Believer, he has an "intense commitment" to certain opinions and groups, is active, gives a portion of his life to his beliefs.

History has required the zealot and the mass movement to break the bonds of tradition. Hoffer says "Christianity was a civilizing and modernizing influence among the savage tribes of Europe. The Crusades and the Reformation both were crucial factors in shaking the Western world from the stagnation of the Middle Ages. In modern times, the mass movements involved in the realization of vast and rapid change are revolutionary and nationalist. . . . The phenomenal modernization of Japan would probably not have been possible without the revivalist spirit of Japanese nationalism."[2] Such movements embody ideologies and utopian hopes, but, says Daniel Bell, there is now "an end to chiliastic hopes, to millenarianism, to apocalyptic thinking—and to ideology. For ideology, which once was a road to action, has come to a dead end."[3] In America, the Populist, the socialist, the Social Darwinist, the Liberty Leaguer, even the technocrat, the union militant, the Black Legionnaire, the Ham and Egger, the Townsendite all are dead or dying. Granted the Black Muslim, granted the southern racist, the John Birchers—they represent in scores what once was a field populated by thousands. And in their place, as monitors of society and agents of social change, there stand the Concerned Citizens.

If this is true, we must know more about this situation, for several reasons, one of which is the possibility that along with some members of the British Commonwealth and the Scandinavian nations, we are developing a political style and a variety of mass opinion appropriate to a new and different phase of history. Our interest here lies with the emotional commitment of the Concerned Citizens in this transitional phase. First, then, it behooves us to examine the nature of this emotional commitment, to see what a Concerned Citizen is concerned about. Second, we shall briefly review some of the more immediate sources of this concern. Third, we must examine the deeper social and psychological factors which might account for both the absence of fanaticism and the presence of concern—a two-edged problem. And fourth, we will look at a special aspect of this distribution of intensity, the problem raised by an intense minority confronted by an indifferent majority.

[1] See Eric Hoffer, *The True Believer* (New York: Mentor, 1958).
[2] *Ibid.,* pp. 14–15.
[3] Daniel Bell, *The End of Ideology* (New York: The Free Press of Glencoe, 1960), p. 370.

The Problem of Intensity

O'Hara, the Eastport maintenance man whom we met in the first chapter, feels strongly about the way President Eisenhower "allowed the recession to come along."[4] Examining his discussion of the way he feels, we find that he was (1) interested in the problem; (2) concerned about it; he (3) feels strongly that the government should give out more defense contracts in his area; he is (4) partisan in his opposition to Republicans in general and to President Eisenhower in particular; and he is (5) certain (has conviction) that the Republicans could do something about it if they wanted to. Let us take these in order.

Interest is "a sense that giving attention to some phenomenon is rewarding,"[5] and by this index there are many concerned citizens in America. Asked "Would you say that you have been very much interested, somewhat interested, or not much interested in following the political campaign so far this year (1952)" 71 per cent of the American public said they were either very much or somewhat interested.[6] Compared with the French, Americans report themselves much more interested in their elections: "three to four times as many Americans say during Presidential elections, that they are 'very' interested" and this difference, while smaller, is still marked when we look at attitudes during congressional elections in non-presidential years.[7] In both countries, of course, interest in public affairs, or special areas of public affairs such as foreign policy, tends to fall off rather markedly compared with the interest in elections.

Concern. A man may be interested without being concerned, and indeed some small fraction of the American public say they are interested in elections but report that they "don't personally care very much which party wins" and even more people don't think the election outcome makes much difference to the country one way or the other.[8] Concern implies that there is some value at stake in a situation, some gain in a preferred outcome; it is future-oriented, while an interest may apply only to the pleasures of the moment. It is central to our Concerned Citizen.

Opinion strength. When a Concerned man makes up his mind (he may be ambivalent for a while; he may be uncertain), he develops opinions which matter to him because they reflect this concern. He will agree or disagree strongly; that is, his opinions will have strength. In general this kind of intensity is measured by a Likert scale, a form of question

[4] O'Hara is one of the men in Lane's *Political Ideology: Why the American Common Man Believes What He Does* (New York: The Free Press of Glencoe, 1962).

[5] Robert E. Lane, *Political Life: Why People Get Involved in Politics* (New York: The Free Press of Glencoe, 1959), p. 133.

[6] Angus Campbell, Gerald Gurin, Warren E. Miller, *The Voter Decides* (Evanston, Ill.: Row, Peterson, 1954), p. 34. Apparently this degree of interest was about the same in 1956. See Angus Campbell, Philip E. Converse, Warren E. Miller, and Donald E. Stokes, *The American Voter* (New York: Wiley, 1960), p. 103.

[7] Philip E. Converse and Georges Dupeux, "Politicization of the Electorate in France and the United States," *Public Opinion Quarterly*, Vol. 26 (1962), p. 4.

[8] Campbell, Gurin, and Miller, *op. cit.*, pp. 36, 38.

The Problem of Intensity

asking about some stated position whether the respondents "agree strongly, not very strongly, not sure, disagree but not very strongly, or disagree strongly." In 1956 the Survey Research Center asked this kind of question on a wide range of issues; the outcome gives us a picture of the areas of more intense concern in the public-opinion firmament. In examining these data the late V. O. Key presents information on the "per cent of total sample with strong opinions"—both agree and disagree, from which we can compile a list of areas of intense feeling.

Table 7   ISSUES IN 1956 WITH HIGH AND LOW DEGREES OF INTENSITY

Selected Issues	Percentage of Total Sample with Strong Opinions
High intensity issues	
Integration	64%
Job guarantees	60
Acting tough toward Russia & China	59
Isolationism	58
Federal aid to education	57
Due process in firing communist suspects	57
Low intensity issues	
Influence of big business	46
Public power and housing	45
Tax cuts	44
Economic aid to foreign nations	37
Aid to neutrals	33

Source: V. O. Key, *Public Opinion and American Democracy* (New York: Knopf, 1961), pp. 213–18.

Partisanship. Not every issue is characterized by conflict; for example, during and just after the war some 96 per cent of the American public stated a belief that there is a God (whereas about 80 per cent of the Czechoslovakian public believed this) (AIPO 11/15/44, CZIPO July, 1946). But where there is a conflict, and therefore parties to the conflict, we may say that an opinion strongly favoring one side is *partisan.* In an election situation, partisanship often follows interest, for an interest tends to "develop" a person's group loyalties and latent predispositions as the chemical developer reveals the picture in the photographic negative.[9] Once a salient partisan loyalty is enlisted, often other opinions "fall into line"; in Norway and much of Europe, class identification is the salient partisan crystallizer of opinion; in the United States it is party loyalty.[10]

Consonance. Partisanship is one emotion; when partisan attitudes are consonant with one another that emotion is intensified. From a variety of sources, it appears to be the case that lack of inner opinion conflict

[9] Paul F. Lazarsfeld, Bernard Berelson, and Hazel Gaudet, *The People's Choice* (New York: Columbia University Press, 1948), pp. 71–86.
[10] Angus Campbell and Henry Valen, "Party Identification in Norway and the United States," *Public Opinion Quarterly*, Vol. 25 (1961), pp. 505–525.

The Problem of Intensity

leads to greater emotional commitment and the kinds of behavior which this implies.[11] Conflict-free commitment is a quality as well as a source of intensity. In an election situation, the more a person's issue, candidate, and party preferences line up on one side the more intensely partisan he becomes, the more he cares about the outcome, the more likely he is to participate.[12] The same thing is true of intensity of belief on other issues.

Conviction. As V. O. Key pointed out, intensity of opinion "may be simply an assurance founded on knowledge."[13] It is generally true that the better-educated hold their opinions more strongly than do the less well-educated; it is as though they felt they had a better right to their opinions. Intensity and certainty go together. Moreover, there is a circularity of emotional commitments: interest leads to knowledge, "knowledge leads to concern, while concern leads to a receptivity to information."[14]

O'Hara is a modestly Concerned Citizen; he is no True Believer. How does he differ therefrom? In the first place, he is interested in his work, family, coaching a boys' baseball team—indeed his interests are more varied than a True Believer's. One might almost say of him that his work in the Little League was his "true belief." Politics and public affairs occupy a much smaller part of his attention span. He has not one, but multiple interests. Second, his level of concern is relative, not total; for the True Believer, everything rides on the success or failure of the "Movement," but for O'Hara, when the Republicans won, he shrugged and said "Well, the Democrats make mistakes, too. Eisenhower may be a good man." Third, he does not use his political, religious, or ethnic opinions to serve as the sole criterion for including or excluding others: he has friends among all groups. This is a matter of principle with him. He is not, in Rokeach's sense, opinionated.[15] His partisanship is more limited. Fourth, he has convictions; there are certain things he thinks he knows but he reports that on all matters it is better to hear two sides than one: his knowledge is not absolute and for all time. He even questions part of his own church's doctrine, although he thinks of himself as a good church member. The True Believer is future-oriented, but O'Hara lives partly for pleasure in the present; he enjoys his family, sports—life now. And yet, he is active in his union, supports the urban redevelopment in his town, votes and talks politics at the shop, cares what happens. He is good for a stable society; but he could never crack the cake of custom or change the social order. That must be done by others.

To appraise, control, understand these varieties of emotional commitments we need to know something of their causes. We turn now to this inquiry.

[11] See, for example, Lazarsfeld, Berelson, and Gaudet, *op. cit.,* pp. 52–64.

[12] Campbell, Converse, Miller, and Stokes, *op. cit.,* pp. 64–97.

[13] V. O. Key, *Public Opinion and American Democracy* (New York: Knopf, 1961), p. 227.

[14] M. Brewster Smith, "The Personal Setting of Public Opinions: A Study of Attitudes Toward Russia," *Public Opinion Quarterly,* Vol. 11 (1947–48), p. 515.

[15] See Milton Rokeach, *The Open and Closed Mind* (New York: Basic Books, 1960), pp. 80–87.

The Problem of Intensity

We have two problems: (1) What kinds of situations produce intense opinions in the opinion market today? (2) How shall we account for a political style which seems, with some exceptions, to generate a capacity for interest, concern, partisanship without fanaticism, true-belief, total commitment? On the first of these, Key offers some interesting information and some sage advice. First, he says, pure self-interest leads to more intense opinions; for example, students feel much more strongly about compulsory chapel in college than do adults who don't have to go to it. Second, group identification leads to more intense feeling on an issue: union members who feel close to their unions have more intense opinions on unions in politics than do those members who have not this sense of close union-identification. Third, general social values, such as the importance of education, generate a pattern of intensity which is not dependent on special advantages and self-interest and may even conflict with them. This is reflected by the lack of relationship between intensity of support for education and having children of school age in the family. Fourth, a special kind of "self-interest," contained in a sense of threat implied by some proposed policy, may affect intensity but not direction of opinion. Thus, although the per cent agreeing to questions on government's responsibility for protecting Negroes does not vary with the proportion of Negroes in a community, the intensity of support declines with an increase in the proportion of Negroes living in the white respondent's community. Finally, intensity of opinion seems to be part of a general pattern of political involvement and concern; each issue borrows significance and probably partisan implications from a more general interest and partisanship. These data lead Key to say, "Intensity of opinion seems by and large to develop when persons are confronted by issues or circumstances that might be expected . . . to arouse their concern most deeply."[16]

We might ask, as Smith, Bruner, and White do, "Of what use to a man are his opinions?" If we knew the answer to that, we would know the sources of interest, concern, partisanship, and conviction of O'Hara's views. Smith and his associates answer their own question by saying that a man's opinions serve (1) to orient him in an instrumental way in the world—that is, to help him get what he wants; (2) they serve to help him adjust to his associates; and (3) they help him to externalize and express his inner conflicts.[17] In the broadest sense, these functions of an opinion help a person to relate to nature and the impersonal world, to other people, and to himself. These seem to be exhaustive, and other functions, such as the immediate gratification involved in expressive acts, and the reinforcement of moral control mechanisms in the self and others,[18] come within

[16] Key, op. cit., pp. 219–227. The quotation is from p. 227.
[17] M. Brewster Smith, Jerome S. Bruner, and Robert W. White, Opinions and Personality (New York: Wiley, 1956), pp. 1, 39–44.
[18] For example, Talcott Parsons distinguishes the expressive, the instrumental, and the moral gratifications in his The Social System (New York: The Free Press of Glencoe, 1951), p. 59.

their scope. As these functions serve intensely felt needs, so opinions will be intense and a man's emotional commitment suitably greater.

But Key's framework is too narrow and Smith and associates' answers too general to explain our national pattern of controlled intensity. Why does this intensity not spill over into fanaticism? Why, in the end, is it compatible with adjustment to frustration and defeat?

Intensity without Fanaticism

Historical epoch. In the first place, looking at the problem with the sweep of history in perspective, we can see that the United States has now passed through a set of "standard" crises which seem to stir the emotions of men to a feverish intensity whenever, in the course of national development, they may occur. We achieved our independence through a war which "stirred men's souls." Our establishment of a constitution was more easily agreed upon than might have been expected; but then it was foreshadowed by the institutions we had lived under during our colonial period. The problem of unification brought about one of the bloodiest civil wars of history, and is not yet forgotten among the defeated citizens of the South. We have never had religious wars, though we have had theocracy and much religious persecution, and the problems of the relations of church and state still evoke some intensity. Even so, these issues are still not so evocative here as in some other nations, where clericalism and anti-clericalism frame one of the main unresolved issues. The question of the distribution of income and property was eased by a great historic prosperity, but the Greenbackers, the Populists, the socialists, and the heritage and unfinished business of the New Deal show a record and a persistence of intense feeling. Today, beyond all others, the race problem stirs men to violent emotion—but in its most intense form only in the South.

The first and most important answer to the question of whence the controlled intensity and partisanship of American politics spring is to be found in this review of history. We have been through some stirring crises; we may have others in store, but at the moment, as the first of the "new nations" we have won through to a period of respite—with the important exception of the race issue. Latent True Believers must await history's call.

Social cleavage. Issues that evoke intense feelings imply social cleavages; social groups with strong identities and loyalties imply divisive issues. The other side of the question of the great historic issues is, then, the question of hostile social groups, and three of the most important of these are class, religion, and race.

(1) *Class.* About one-third of the people in the nation have indicated that they never think of themselves as belonging to a social class (even though they would name "their" class when pressed), and for this group class identification is largely unrelated to political choice. Social class is not a political reference group, even an unconscious one, for this third of a nation. For the others, those who sometimes think of themselves in class terms, the relationship between class identification and political choice declined continuously from 1948 to 1956. Moreover, the impor-

tance of class identification for orienting people on certain ideological issues, such as the proper role of the welfare state, also declined steadily over this period.[19] As noted above, compared with Norway (and presumably other European countries), social class in the United States is not a reference group upon which intense partisan feeling can be built.[20]

(2) *Religion*. There is a Catholic-Protestant tension in the United States;[21] the assimilation process has not so reduced the differential association as to obliterate differences in political loyalties;[22] there are persistent substantive issues which divide Catholics from Protestants. Given this state of affairs, the apparent historic *change* of divisive attitudes relevant to this form of cleavage is as important as the current state of conflict. For the Catholic, the idea that a Catholic communicant could not be President has been an important symbolic issue since 1928; today this has been removed and with it a shriveling of certain religious political differences. The relative religious-political alignment has changed recently in such a way as to imply a rapprochement. This is revealed in Tables 8a and 8b. The "difference" figures themselves do not measure religious-political cleavages, since they mask class and urbanism factors as well. Moreover, the candidates are not the same in each case. However, compared with one another they suggest important changes over time; the 1960–1963 comparison involves, in each year, a Catholic running against a Protestant. It suggests, tentatively at least, the declining impact of religion on political

Table 8a   WOULD YOU VOTE FOR A CATHOLIC FOR PRESIDENT?

Year	Yes	No	Undecided
1940	62%	31%	7%
1958	68	25	7
1959	69	20	11
1960	71	20	9
1961	82	13	5
1963	84	13	3

Source: AIPO 10/4/63.

Table 8b   CATHOLIC AND PROTESTANT SUPPORT for Democratic Party Ticket, 1956, 1960, 1963

Year	Catholic Support for Democratic Ticket; % of Two-Party Vote	Protestant Support for Democratic Ticket; % of Two-Party Vote	Difference
1956	51	37	14
1960	78	38	40
1963* (April)	86	58	28

* Kennedy *vs.* Rockefeller
Source: AIPO 10/30/60, 4/7/63.

[19] Campbell, Converse, Miller, and Stokes, *op. cit.,* pp. 343–349.

[20] Campbell and Valen, *op. cit.*

[21] John L. Kane, "Protestant-Catholic Tensions," *American Sociological Review,* Vol. 16 (1951), pp. 663–672.

[22] Scott Greer, "Catholic Voters and the Democratic Party," *Public Opinion Quarterly,* Vol. 25 (1961), pp. 611–625.

The Problem of Intensity

choice; the difference has moved about halfway toward the 1956 situation, which, incidentally, was one in which Catholic-Protestant differences were historically low. This view is supported by the finding in Elmira in 1948 that the sons of Catholics were more Republican than their fathers and the sons of Protestants were more Democratic than their fathers.[23]

Nor is this (rather modest) rapprochement limited to strictly electoral issues. In recent times the issue of public aid to Catholic schools has been divisive, but differences between religious groups have declined:

Table 9   PERCENTAGE APPROVING FEDERAL AID
to Catholic and Other Private Schools 1961, 1963, by Religion

Group	1963	1961
Protestants	42%	29%
Catholics	71	66
Difference	29	37

Source: AIPO 2/10/63.

(3) *Race.* There is reason to believe that in some quarters the intensity of opinions on racial matters is growing, and as we reported, it is the issue on which there was the highest ratio of "strong" to "not so strong" opinions on each side of the segregation issue in 1960. Yet there is some evidence of a set of opposing forces working to de-intensify the group partisanship—and this in the South, as well. Among these forces are the influence of the national media, the changed attitudes that come with increased urbanization, and the demands of the Negroes, themselves.

The dramatic increase in the per cent of the Southern public anticipating the success of the integration movement may be ephemeral (the Birmingham riots later in 1963 had a marked effect on public opinion), but together with the long-term increase in Southern white support for desegregation they suggest one reason why the True Believers of the Ku Klux Klan and the Black Muslims have not been in possession of the field of battle.

Permanence of issues. Intensity of loyalty to a party or a union or even

Table 10   WHITE SOUTHERN VIEWS ON RACE RELATIONS IN 1942 AND 1956

White South Only	1942	1956
Approve school integration	2%	14%
Approve integration of transportation	4	27
Do not object to residential proximity	12	38

Source: Herbert H. Hyman and Paul B. Sheatsley, "Attitudes Toward Desegregation," *Scientific American,* Vol. 195 (1956, pp. 36–37).

[23] Bernard R. Berelson, Paul F. Lazarsfeld, and William N. McPhee, *Voting* (Chicago: University of Chicago Press, 1954), p. 70.

The Problem of Intensity

a class or religion seems to be a product of the span of years a person has experienced that loyalty.[24] The same may be true of an opinion about other matters: the longer an opinion is held the more intense the feeling associated with it. But in a modern society, and particularly in the United States, issues come and go with a bewildering rapidity. Whereas, for example, the issue of socialism is an old story in Europe and men have grown up with their socialist or anti-socialist beliefs, the American equivalent, the welfare state, is an issue which dates back in its broad modern form only to the New Deal, and in that guise is hardly controversial any more. In a society where issues tend to emerge as ad hoc responses to specific problems, and the mental set of the people is such as to encourage their perception as such, devoid of an ideological superstructure,[25] issues rarely acquire this enduring quality. Hence they rarely acquire that intensity of feeling which comes with long acquaintance and partisanship.

Table 11   CHANGING SOUTHERN ESTIMATES OF RACE RELATIONS, 1957–1963

"Do you think the day will ever come in the South when whites and Negroes will be going to the same schools, eating in the same restaurants, and generally sharing the same public accommodations?"

Date	Yes	No	Uncertain
August 1957	45%	33%	22%
October 1958	53	31	16
January 1961	76	19	5
July 1963	83	13	4

Source: AIPO 7/19/63.

Frustration. Fanaticism thrives on frustration with the old order and an abandonment of hope that it will offer relief. "For men to plunge headlong into an undertaking of vast change, they must be intensely discontented";[26] they must feel that their homes and farms are in jeopardy, their religious practices threatened, their national identity impugned. But a comparison of attitudes in eight modern Western nations and Mexico shows that Americans rank fairly high, generally third or fourth, in their satisfaction with "how they are getting on" in life, with the Australians and the Norwegians, generally ahead of them, and the British and the Dutch generally about the same. Moreover, in the United States, compared with other nations, the levels of satisfaction[27] were most nearly equalized among the various status and occupational groups; there was a kind of equality of satisfaction embracing owners and workers alike. Although there is no evidence that Americans are psychologically healthier than others, it does seem that a sense of political frustration and alienation does not develop

[24] Campbell, Converse, Miller, and Stokes, *op. cit.,* pp. 323–327.
[25] See Lane, *Political Ideology,* pp. 346–363.
[26] Hoffer, *op. cit.,* p. 20.
[27] Alex Inkeles, "Industrial Man: The Relation of Status to Experience, Perception, and Value," *American Journal of Sociology,* Vol. 66 (1960), pp. 1–31.

The Problem of Intensity

because, in general, American men feel that their lives are more or less satisfying. There is no need for "a desperate clinging to something which might give worth and meaning to our futile, spoiled lives,"[28] because men did not see their lives as futile or spoiled. And in the United States, as in England and Norway, there is no need to hate a scapegoated group or love a charismatic leader who promises radical change—two of the great sources of fanatical emotion in politics.

Public and private spheres. What we are talking about is the intensity of opinion on public and primarily political matters, matters which usually come to a focus in government action. If it should be the case that politics in the United States occupied a smaller sphere of the attention orbit than is the case in other countries, another reason for the lack of intense emotional investment in political questions would come into view. The matter is not easy to decide. In addition, it must be observed that Americans hold more elections for more offices than any other nation; they employ the initiative and referendum more than any other country (with the possible exception of Switzerland); they tend to join political organizations to about the same extent as the French and attend only slightly fewer political rallies than they do. On the other hand, Americans attempt to influence others politically rather more than the French. (The relatively lower voting turnout seems to be a product of more stringent registration requirements, rather than lower interest.)[29] Americans are not apolitical. On the other hand, observers have often commented on the lower American level of political partisanship. For example, Bernard Barber refers to certain kinds of political apathy as being the product of "the pre-eminence of occupational and kinship-role obligations in American society" and their divorce from political life.[30]

The problem, we think, is partially resolved by considering the special style of political and social involvement in the United States. Compared with others, Americans seem to regard public affairs as an equally important but more limited sphere of life. And in a cross-cultural comparison of values, Charles Morris finds that compared with students in India, Japan, China, and Norway, students in the United States "seem to wish most of all to be flexible and many-sided. They show less restraint than the Indian students and *less commitment to social causes than do the Chinese or Indian students.* But [the data also] very much show that they do not want to be socially irresponsible."[31] As reported above, McClelland found that American students, compared with German students, participate more in voluntary groups, yet they have a smaller sense of obligation to society and a greater sense of obligation to develop themselves.[32] This pattern of

28 Hoffer, *op. cit.,* p. 24.

29 Converse and Dupeux, *op. cit.,* pp. 4–9.

30 Bernard Barber, "Participation and Mass Apathy in Associations," in Alvin W. Gouldner (ed.), *Studies in Leadership* (New York: Harper, 1950), p. 478.

31 Charles Morris, *Varieties of Human Value* (Chicago: University of Chicago Press, 1956), p. 50.

32 David C. McClelland, *The Achieving Society* (Princeton: Van Nostrand, 1961), p. 198.

The Problem of Intensity

social and political participation, combined with a relatively higher focus on self-advancement, self-indulgence and self-development, may contribute to our understanding of the sources of involvement without fanaticism, of commitment with a capacity for adjustment. The sphere of government and politics is, so to speak, balanced off against a weightier private sphere.

Extremity. One of the best established patterns of public opinion is the U-shaped relationship between extremity on some substantive issue (such as the degree of Negro integration desired, or the degree of regulation desired for industry) and intensity of feeling. The more extreme the stand, the more intensely do people feel about it. In the above illustration, the most integrationist position and the most segregationist position would be held most intensely; and those in the middle, the moderates, would be relatively less emotionally committed.[33] This is so well established, in fact, that in searching for a "zero" position on an issue scale, researchers will choose the position on which people feel least strongly, "folding" as they say, the scale at that point.[34] Speculation on this relationship has produced a number of ideas: Allport and Hartman suggest that extremists are usually taking a more selective view of a situation and must devote energy (emotional intensity) to screening out opposing considerations. Lying behind this selectivity, they say, there are often repressed emotional drives; the intensity and assertion of their opinions are employed to help in this repression.[35] On a more common-sense level, Cantril argues that those who are on the defensive because of their extreme views must either develop an intensity of feeling or else succumb to community pressures to moderate their views. Thus those who remain extremists represent what is left over after those who might adopt an extreme position, for a variety of reasons, have been winnowed and the less intense partisans and the emotionally less active have been culled from the group.[36]

But there are other grounds, as well. One way of being moderate is to believe that "there is something to be said on both sides." In a study of attitudes toward the teachers' oath in California, Wilner and Fearing found that those who answered *both* of the following questions in either a pro-oath or an anti-oath position tend to report themselves as being more "certain" of their stand, more "interested" in the problem, and having a better "understanding" of it:

Are you in favor of requiring all faculty members on this campus to sign a loyalty oath which includes a declaration that the individual is not a member of the Communist Party?

[33] Hadley Cantril, "The Intensity of an Attitude," *Journal of Abnormal and Social Psychology,* Vol. 41 (1946), pp. 129–135.

[34] Edward A. Suchman, "The Intensity Component in Attitude and Opinion Research," in Samuel A. Stouffer and others (eds.), "Measurement and Prediction," Vol. 4 of *Studies in Social Psychology in World War II* (Princeton: Princeton University Press, 1950), pp. 213–276.

[35] Floyd H. Allport and D. A. Hartman, "Measurement and Motivation of Atypical Opinions in a Certain Group," *American Political Science Review,* Vol. 19 (1925), pp. 735–760.

[36] Cantril, *op. cit.*

Do you favor dismissing from the university, faculty members who refuse to sign such a loyalty oath?

But about an eighth of the sample answered the first question "yes" and the second question "no," and this group of "fence-straddlers" had a lower sense of conviction and were less interested in the issue, two measures of emotional intensity.[37] Moderation can imply conflict, or dissonance, and conflict and dissonance often tend to be handled psychologically by a withdrawal of emotion. As we said earlier, consonance is an important ingredient in intense partisanship. Because of their geographic and social mobility, Americans may tend to be placed more often than other nationals in such conflict positions, where there is more dissonance than consonance.

Finally, there is something congenial between extremity and intensity which suggests a mutual support. For example, among democratic (nonauthoritarian) samples, there is a tendency for those who are most extreme in their equalitarianism to be most militant in the advocacy of their position.[38] The forces nourishing extremity seem also to nourish the intensity.

It might be the case that a people had a general preference for extremist views, preferring to distinguish themselves in exotic ways, or voting "far left" without a commitment to a leftist program because it represents an extreme, or preferring splinter parties which differentiate one's position from the great middle. But in America it seems not to be that way. This is apparent not only in the voting patterns, but also in studies of opinions on a range of issues. Cantril shows that on attitudes on government policy toward business, the middle position (with the lowest intensity) is the most frequently chosen; although usually on an extremity (Thurstone) scale there is not a normal curve, with the most popular choices in the middle, there is a tendency for the extremes to be less chosen than some more moderate position. Extremity is, then, associated with *deviance,* and all of the forces of conformity and "other-directedness" discussed above are mobilized to bring Americans away from the wings and toward the center. This moves them at once away from the areas of intense feeling to the area of more moderate and manageable emotion.

Socialization. One source of intensity in politics is a socialization (maturation) process which somehow invests this area of life with special emotional significance. One could imagine that this would come about in two different ways: (1) parents themselves moralize political choices and these are internalized by the growing child, or (2) children rebel against their parents and employ political difference as a vehicle of rebellion. On the first point, it appears from Greenstein's work that politics is little talked about in the American home, that the children absorb a party identification without many supporting attitudes or much information, and that children's earliest disposition is to think of government in terms of a "benevo-

[37] Daniel M. Wilner and Franklin Fearing, "The Structure of Opinion: A 'Loyalty Oath' Poll," *Public Opinion Quarterly,* Vol. 14 (1950–51), p. 742.
[38] Lawrence A. Dombrose and Daniel J. Levinson, "Ideological 'Militancy' and 'Pacificism' in Democratic Individuals," *Journal of Social Psychology,* Vol. 32 (1950), pp. 101–113.

The Problem of Intensity

lent leader" who looks after his people.[39] This is not the material out of which fanaticism, or even marked deviance, is developed. Lane's material on the memories of politics in the home possessed by working-class men supports this view.[40] On the second point, the political rebellion of American adolescents, the findings of a recent study by Middleton and Putney show that although there is considerable (but, still, easily contained) generalized adolescent rebellion, this has almost nothing to do with political deviance from parental political positions. On the other hand, those who do not "feel close" to their parents are more likely to rebel politically, but this turns out to be important only if the parents were seen as interested in politics, thus making political rebellion "worthwhile." Yet, on the whole, the authors of this study agree with Hyman in that "political attitudes in America are not in general generated by adolescent rebellion" and the role of other factors seem to them to be more important.[41] Moreover, students tend to feel closer to parents who are seen as interested in politics (because the socially involved adult is a better parent or because parents who communicate an interest to their children create this kind of closeness?)—an unexpected finding which suggests that the awakening of political interests is more likely to be done in a beneficent home environment where parental ties are strong. It seems this sheds light on an important influence shaping the involved but unfanatical participant in political life.

Daniel Bell, who, as we noted above, claims the end of ideology is here, concludes that the politics of our era has changed, there has been an exhaustion of new political ideas, a decline of social movements, a tendency no longer for ideas to serve as levers for action. "What gives ideology its force," he says, "is its passion" and this is spent.[42] Bell is disappointed and believes that the intellectuals of the West are both disappointed and angry because the springs of ideology have run dry and questions of technique have come to the fore to take their place. But what this suggests for the United States and other Western nations is that the "True Believer," the mass man in a mass movement, is (temporarily?) dead as well. What we have been exploring here are the wellsprings of that other source of interest and action, controlled and patient emotion, disciplined by experience, surely in the modern nations a better foundation for a better society.

The Political Consequences of the Intensity Pattern

We have been discussing these things as though there were only one important matter—namely, the control and rationalization of intensely felt

[39] Fred I. Greenstein, "The Benevolent Leader: Children's Images of Political Authority," *American Political Science Review*, Vol. 54 (1960), pp. 934–943.

[40] Robert E. Lane, "Fathers and Sons: Foundations of Political Belief," *American Sociological Review*, Vol. 24 (1959), pp. 502–511.

[41] Russell Middleton and Snell Putney, "Political Expression of Adolescent Rebellion," *American Journal of Sociology*, Vol. 68 (1963), pp. 527–535; quotation on p. 534. See also Herbert Hyman, *Political Socialization* (New York: The Free Press of Glencoe, 1959).

[42] Bell, *op. cit.*, p. 371.

The Problem of Intensity

opinions in the political game. But the social distribution of these emotions is important as well. On this point Berelson says:

> How could a mass democracy work if all the people were deeply involved in politics? . . . Extreme interest goes with extreme partisanship and might culminate in rigid fanaticism that could destroy the democratic process if generalized throughout the community. . . . Low interest provides maneuvering room for political shifts necessary for a complex society in a period of rapid change . . . Hence, an important balance between action motivated by strong sentiments and action with little passion behind it is obtained by heterogeneity within the electorate.[43]

But he does not say where the balance should lie and it is important.

One of the aspects of this problem is most cogently raised by Robert Dahl in his discussion of the relation of democratic theory to the social distribution of intense opinions.[44] He postulates several circumstances, which are best understood by a series of figures. The first of these is a strong consensus marked by strong preferences, as shown in Fig. 1. Here most people strongly prefer one alternative policy and there is no conflict between majority rule and minority intensity. Neither is there in a situation where most people rather weakly prefer one alternative, as shown in Fig. 2. Figure 3 shows a situation where opinion is about evenly divided but the intensity of opinion is low and the "injustice" in a decision for either group is not great; nor would there be much sense of grievance if the distribution of opinion were tilted one way or the other. Now we come to a situation in which there is a strong and intense feeling on each side, and the sides are about the same in size, as shown in Fig. 4. Relatively few people are indifferent, and those who care a great deal about some policy decision are about equally divided. This is the situation which Dahl thinks characterized public opinion just before the Civil War. And if the issue is crucial, as it seemed to be in that case, it may presage the breakdown of democratic government. Finally, there is the situation which poses the most difficult problem of equity, the indifferent majority and the intense minority, shown in Fig. 5. Relating this to the problem of minority rights, Dahl finds that most of the devices designed to protect minorities do so without regard to whether or not the majority has equally intense preferences and, in any event, tend to protect rich and powerful minorities at the expense of weak minorities, such as Negroes and sharecroppers. Dahl believes that most controversies in a stable democracy are best described by variations of the situations portrayed in Figs. 1, 2, and 3; but the problem of the intense minority bothers him as it did Madison.

Looking at V. O. Key's calculations of "intensity ratios" on a range of issues (measured by a ratio between "strongly agree" and "agree not so strongly" = intensity of agreement, and "strongly disagree" and "disagree not so strongly" = intensity of disagreement) let us see how intense opin-

[43] Berelson, Lazarsfeld, and McPhee, op. cit., pp. 314–315.
[44] Robert A. Dahl, A Preface to Democratic Theory (Chicago: University of Chicago Press, 1956), pp. 90–119.

The Problem of Intensity

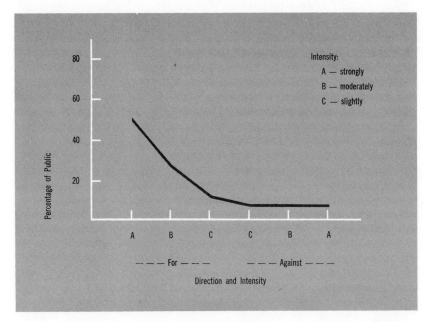

FIGURE 1. *Strong consensus with strong preferences.* (Source: Robert A. Dahl, *A Preface to Democratic Theory* (Chicago: Phoenix Publications, University of Chicago, 1963), pp. 93, 94.

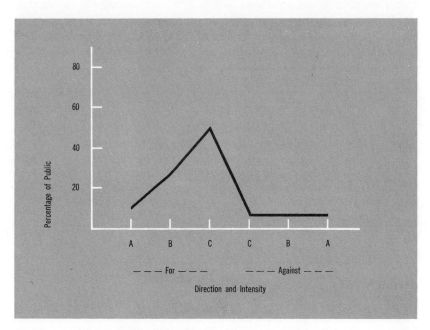

FIGURE 2. *Strong consensus with weak preferences.* (Source: Dahl, *op. cit.,* pp. 93, 94.)

The Problem of Intensity

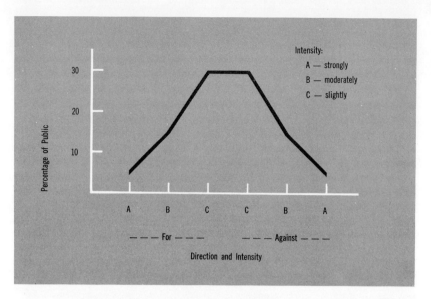

FIGURE 3. *Opinion about evenly divided; weak preferences.* (Source: Dahl, *op. cit.*, pp. 93, 94.)

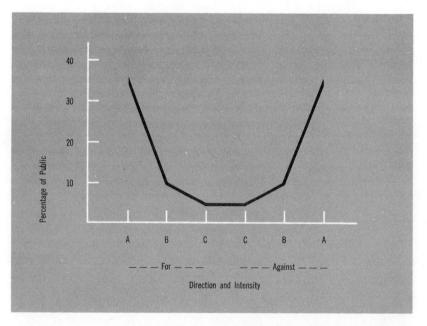

FIGURE 4. *Opinion about evenly divided; strong preferences.* (Source: Dahl, *op. cit.*, pp. 98, 99.)

The Problem of Intensity

ions fit into Dahl's several models.[45] From these data we learn several things. In the first place, in only three out of 32 instances are there more people with moderate "agree" or "disagree" opinions than intense ones. This means that in almost every case the situations tend to resemble Dahl's explosive model as represented by Fig. 4, except that instead of U-shaped, they tend to be J-shaped, because there are more intense opinions on one side than the other. Yet, when we look, not at the intensity of reported feeling but at the substance of the questions, only one question seems to reflect an explosive situation: "The government in Washington should stay out of the question of whether white and colored children go to the same school." We must remind ourselves, as Key does on several occasions, that "intensity" of opinion has many meanings. Specifically it is not the same as *cruciality*, which might be defined as an opinion for which a person is likely to sacrifice his ordinary support of law and order.

The second point is that among the 16 issues on which we have data, there are *no* instances of the problem which bothered Dahl: an indifferent majority and an intense minority, although there are two instances of the reverse: an intense majority and a relatively indifferent minority, each dealing with aspects of foreign policy on which there were relatively high numbers of no opinion responses. But is it true that the problem of an indifferent majority and an intense minority disappears for want of cases in the real world? So far the evidence is not conclusive because of the general tendency to choose the more intense "strongly agree (disagree)" option. Taking into account the tendency of people to agree and disagree "strongly," discounting for this, we can look for situations where there is a higher intensity ratio in the minority than in the majority, making for a *relatively* more intense minority than majority. Examining the sixteen issues we find only one instance where this is the case ("The United States should give economic help to the poorer countries of the world even if they can't pay for it," agree 43%, no opinion 17%, disagree 40%; agree intensity ratio: .99; disagree intensity ratio 1.67). It is an issue on which feeling runs low and on which the two sides are almost evenly divided. Our conclusion must be that even taking *relative* intensity into account, on political issues with a broad public, there are very few cases where there is an indifferent majority and an intense minority. On more highly specialized issues (the wool tariff, an airport in New Haven) of course, there will often be intense minorities; this is indeed the world of the special interests: but in their world they very often win.

But the problem of the intense minority and the apathetic majority does not disappear. For perhaps it is the case that political parties exhibit this characteristic; that is, perhaps it is the case that Republicans, although in a minority, tend to be intense partisans, whereas Democrats with almost twice as many "members" in the national public, tend to be more apathetic. But this is not the case, either. By a few percentage points there are more "weak" Democrats than "strong" ones (at least there were in 1952 and 1953) and there are almost exactly the same number of weak as

[45] Key, *op. cit.*, pp. 212–218.

The Problem of Intensity

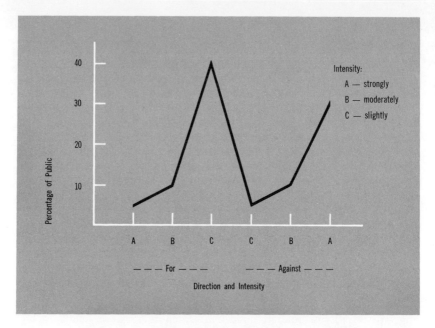

FIGURE 5. *Majority with weak preferences; minority with strong preferences.* (Source: Dahl, *op. cit.,* pp. 98, 99.)

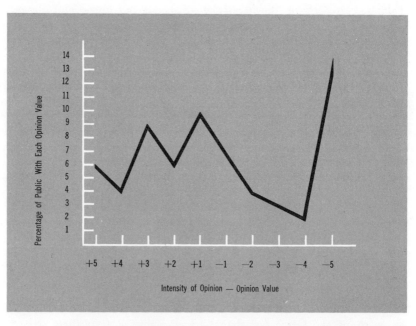

FIGURE 6. *Intensity of support and opposition to Senator McCarthy.* (Source: AIPO 6/24/53.)

The Problem of Intensity

strong Republicans.[46] Little injustice can be read into this picture of the distribution of intense party loyalties.

Finally, we come to the question of intensity of support for political leaders. In the 1952 election, the candidate partisanship scores of the Survey Research Center give us a measure of partisan support (though this may reflect only roughly how strongly people feel about their man). But here again the majority seems more intense. The Eisenhower supporters were more "partisan" than the Stevenson supporters (5% of the population were *strong* Stevenson partisans on this measure; 20% were *strong* Eisenhower partisans).[47] Yet the situation Dahl had in mind does occur with respect to political leaders, as a 1953 survey of attitudes toward McCarthy shows. The AIPO asked a national sample about McCarthy (June 24, 1953), using a special card to show intensity. The interviewers handed the respondents these cards saying: "You notice that the 10 boxes on this card go from the HIGHEST position of plus 5—or something you like very much—to the LOWEST position of minus 5—or something you dislike very much. Will you put your finger on any one of the 10 boxes which best represents your opinion of Senator Joseph E. McCarthy?" The results follow (see also Fig. 6).

Here, at last, we have a clear-cut case of an intense minority and a relatively indifferent majority—but the differences in size and intensity are still not very great. Nevertheless, something of the quality of the political conflict surrounding the Senator may have come from this complexion of support and opposition: a defensive majority ("I like his goals but don't approve of his methods.") and the cornered bitter opposition of his opponents who felt frustrated and angry about their political position. The minority did feel a certain unfairness in the political process which produced this situation, as Dahl said they would. The problem of the relatively indifferent majority and the intense minority is a real one, but in perspective, and on the broad canvas of national issues, parties, and candidates, not a frequent one.

Table 12   INTENSITY OF SUPPORT AND OPPOSITION TO SENATOR McCARTHY, 1953

Value	Percentage at Each Value	Majority and Minority Totals	Average Intensity Score for Majority and Minority
5	6		
4	4		
3	9	Majority pro-McCarthy = 35%	2.7 majority
2	6		
1	10		
−1	7		
−2	4		
−3	3	Minority anti-McCarthy = 30%	3.4 minority
−4	2		
−5	14		
No opinion	35	35	
Total	100	100	

Source: AIPO July 24, 1953.

[46] Campbell, Gurin, and Miller, *op. cit.,* p. 94.

[47] *Ibid.,* p. 140.

The Problem of Intensity

Concluding
Comments

A political system is shaped
and guided by two things: what its members
believe, and the way they learn and change their beliefs.
We have not looked at the complexion
of popular beliefs in this book, but we have examined various
ways in which beliefs and opinions are learned
and changed and some of the associated problems. Without
summarizing this discussion, perhaps we can
illuminate some of its principal themes.

1. A person's political orientations are given an early direction by his family; before he knows much about politics he develops a party identification and then a little later some guide lines for argument, such as his feelings about "the working man," "foreign nations," and political life in his community. The basic *trust* which characterizes the American child's attitude toward government is an important ingredient in the development of future attitudes. Political maturation is a combined process of finding reasons for this early orientation and refining it, on the one hand, and of modifying it so that it "fits" into the changing social environment of the youth and the young adult, on the other.

2. The constellation of group memberships and identifications becomes the basic shaping force in later life, for they guide people in their thinking about themselves and others; by referring to them a person learns what he should believe and why. This is a twofold process: the group memberships and references provide (objective) channels of communications and (subjective) identifications.

3. People identify with individuals, with opinion leaders, as they do with groups. These leaders serve as the main agents of opinion change; but they do so only partly through what they say. Often, as we have seen in the discussion of cognitive dissonance, their effectiveness rests heavily on *who* and *what* they are and on people's response to them as people: often they are people with political histories which they bring to the discussion. The inter-personal sentiments shape the reception of the inter-idea discussion in the specific ways we have discussed.

4. The public is not well informed on current topics; but that handicaps them less than the low level of conceptualization and thought brought to bear on public affairs. Without a framework of appropriate ideas, no amount of civic information will help; but, of course, it is hard to arrive at a fair judgment without some knowledge of what is going on. By pouring civic information and historical knowledge into students, instead of teaching them how to think and analyze social problems, our educational system misses its great opportunity.

5. This problem of political thinking, however, embraces the question of what kind of rational thought is needed. We have argued that, in addition to the usual ideas about logical inference, we must conceive of the rational political man as someone who is not at war with himself, who understands his entire range of needs and values and can decide even topical issues on the basis of this self-information. The "rational man" must be able to keep his wishes from influencing his perceptions and to bear the pain of disagreeable knowledge. Only whole men are, in this sense, reasonable men.

6. Concern for the opinions of others, sensitivity to what they are thinking, we have said, is positively helpful in a democracy and in a developing economy. Although conformity as a rigid doctrine is dysfunctional, a selective conformity may be useful, the capacity to conform is necessary, the willingness to maintain a group loyalty is valuable, and other-directedness combined with a sense of obligation to the self is especially valuable in a democratic system.

115

Concluding Comments

7. In order to break the mold of traditional society, fanatical religious, nationalistic, or reformist sentiments have been necessary; but in a flexible modern society, such fanaticism on a large scale is out of place. What is wanted, instead, is a political style centering on the Concerned Citizen, a person with multiple interests and values who is interested, concerned, and partisan—within more limited bounds. Certain Western nations, including the United States, have developed these adaptive styles, partly because they have passed through certain "standard" historical crises, partly because social cleavages are increasingly diffused, partly because of a kind of transience of social issues, partly because the economy and the social order offer less life frustration, partly because the domain of government is more limited, and partly because children are brought up in certain ways conducive to this non-rebellious political style. Furthermore, it seems that the political system rarely develops that most frustrating situation: an indifferent majority and an intense minority.

The picture is a mixed one, but we do not join the chorus of those who despair over the condition of modern man, who find him hopelessly lost, alienated from his society and government, irrational to the point that his transient needs overwhelm his long-term interests. Most people have a very modest conceptual equipment for the political thinking they do; most are insufficiently informed to rely very much on their own resources for their political decisions; most people on most issues are partisan first and then later discover the reasons for their partisanship. But their partisanship develops, on the whole, out of a family life which binds them in a trusting fashion to society, out of a set of group identifications which combines loyalty with some capacity for criticism, and a set of political "passions" which, on the whole and for the moment, offer a modestly concerned interest in public affairs without the risks of total commitment.

Concluding Comments

To Explore Further . . .

It is difficult in a short book such as this to cover or mention all pertinent writings on a topic. The interested student is therefore well-advised to consult some of the following works on topics which he would like to explore further.

Perhaps the most ambitious effort to describe opinions was made by M. Brewster Smith, Robert W. White, and Jerome S. Bruner in their *Opinions and Personality* (New York: Wiley, 1956). A more thorough effort to investigate the political thinking of Americans may be found in Robert E. Lane, *Political Ideology* (New York: The Free Press of Glencoe, 1962). A recent, systematic approach has been made by Daniel Katz and Ezra Stotland: "A Preliminary Statement to a Theory of Attitude Structure and Change," in S. Koch (ed.), *Psychology: A Study of a Science: Formulations of the Person and the Social Context,* Vol. III (New York: McGraw-Hill, 1959). A standard work on opinion measurement is S. A. Stouffer, et al., *Measurement and Prediction* (Princeton: Princeton University Press, 1950).

An able summary of the evidence on political socialization has been provided by Herbert Hyman in his *Political Socialization* (New York: The Free Press of Glencoe, 1959). This may be supplemented by a new interpretation, supported by an extensive study of children's politics in New Haven, by Fred Greenstein: *Children and Politics* (New Haven: Yale University Press, forthcoming in 1965). For interesting theoretical viewpoints, see also T. M. Newcomb's *Personality and Social Change* (New York: Dryden, 1943); and H. McClosky and H. E. Dahlgren, "Primary Group Influence on Party Loyalty," *American Political Science Review,* Vol. 53 (1959), pp. 757–776.

The most systematic program of research on the effects of mass communications is summarized in a series of monographs edited by the late Carl I. Hovland, and published by the Yale University Press. See especially *Communication and Persuasion* (1953), by C. I. Hovland, I. L. Janis, and H. H. Kelley; and *Attitude Organization and Change* (1960), by M. Rosenberg, C. I. Hovland, et al. The theoretical viewpoints of Festinger, Heider, Newcomb, and Osgood and Tannenbaum are ably summarized and criticized by several writers in a special issue of the *Public Opinion Quarterly,* edited by Daniel Katz, Vol. 24 (Summer, 1960). Those who wish to pursue Leon Festinger's ideas on cognitive dissonance further are referred to his *A Theory of Cognitive Dissonance* (Stanford: Calif.: Stanford University Press, 1957).

Survey data on information have been summarized by Hazel Gaudet Erskine in several issues of the *Public Opinion Quarterly* (Winter, 1962, and Spring and Fall, 1963). A provocative view of the relationship between information and partisan attitudes has been outlined by Philip E. Converse, "Information Flow and the Stability of Partisan Attitudes," *Public Opinion Quarterly,* Vol. 26 (1962), pp. 578–599. The degree of conceptualization and extent of ideologizing in the American public are taken up by A. Campbell, P. E. Converse, W. E. Miller, and D. E. Stokes, in *The American Voter* (New York: Wiley, 1960), especially in Chapters 9 and 10.

The popular literature on conformity has grown beyond any reasonable limit. David Riesman's *The Lonely Crowd* (Garden City, N.Y.: Doubleday Anchor, 1956) is by now a classic, and theories of mass society and the concerns expressed by many about conformity are ably represented by Winston White, *Beyond Conformity* (New York: The Free Press of Glencoe, 1961) and by the discussion in Irving Janis and associates, *Personality and Persuasibility* (New Haven: Yale University Press, 1959).

The problem of distinguishing between a "true believer" with his dogmatic and singleminded adherence to a particular doctrine, and a "concerned citizen" with his strong interest in public affairs, is one that goes far back in political theory. The term itself comes from Eric Hoffer's *The True Believer* (New York: Mentor, 1958). A variety of studies have been done of "true believers," among them those published in *The Radical Right,* edited by Daniel Bell (Garden City, N.Y.: Doubleday, 1963); and in G. Almond's *The Appeals of Communism* (Princeton: Princeton University Press, 1964). Excellent fictional—but realistic—portrayal of communist thinking is revealed in Arthur Koestler's *Darkness at Noon.* For an empirically-oriented effort to grapple with differences in issues and the way they are handled by the American public, see V. O. Key, Jr.'s *Public Opinion and American Democracy* (New York: Knopf, 1961).

For the reader interested in the mass media, we suggest Joseph T. Klapper's *The Effects of Mass Communication* (New York: The Free Press of Glencoe, 1960). The kinds of opinions and circumstances which lead to political participation are summarized and interpreted in Robert E. Lane, *Political Life: Why People Get Involved in Politics* (New York: The Free Press of Glencoe, 1959). And S. M. Lipset develops a variety of interesting ideas on the relationship between opinions and political systems in his *Political Man* (Garden City, N.Y.: Doubleday, 1960).

Index